Learning to Live After the Trauma of a Stroke

The True Story of Officer McSkimming

Dan McSkimming

An Imprint of Sulis International Press
Los Angeles | Dallas | London

LEARNING TO LIVE AFTER A STROKE: THE TRUE STORY OF A POLICE OFFICER
Copyright ©2023 by Dan McSkimming. All rights reserved.

Except for brief quotations for reviews, no part of this book may be reproduced in any form or by any electronic or mechanical means, including information storage and retrieval systems, without written permission from the publisher. Email: info@sulisinternational.com.

Front cover painting by Dan McSkimming,

ISBN (print): 978-1-958139-28-8
ISBN (eBook): 978-1-958139-29-5
Published by Sulis Press
An Imprint of Sulis International
Los Angeles | Dallas | London

www.sulisinternational.com

Contents

Preface 1

The Call to my Wife 5

The Injury at the Chiropractor 9

My Life 13

Emergency Room and Cottage Hospital — August ... 29

Cottage Hospital (September) 49

Mission Terrace/Cottage Rehab (October) 55

Fundraiser 63

Coming Home 65

Divorce 73

On My Own 77

Caregivers 83

Relationships Changes 91

Moving Forward 101

Focusing on the Positive 109

A Final Word 113

Preface

In 2014, I left some dishes in the sink to wash later, and went to a chiropractor's appointment. Little did I know that the visit would change my entire life: I would be wheelchair bound, retired early from the police force, divorced. My whole life was turned upside down forever by the stroke caused by a simple adjustment of the neck from the chiropractor.

I don't recall the end of 2014 lost almost none of 2015. I was in an induced coma for 2 weeks, then spent months in rehabilitation hospitals. Even when I became somewhat alert, I could not speak and had to relearn the basics of living. I had to retire from the police force, and a few months later, my wife filed for divorce.

As a young man at the age of 43, with a lovely wife, two children, a nice home, and a fulfilling career. I was a police Senior Deputy, and a member of the SWAT/SET (Special Weapon and Tactics Team and Special Enforcement Team). I thought I had my life planned out. The sudden loss of *everything* but my life was not only physically demanding, but mentally and emotionally challenging. When you become an invalid, especially in a wheelchair, people often think you are different. But I hadn't changed who I was inside! During much of the initial struggle to relearn how to function and figure out a new life, I sometimes wished I was out of my mind, so I wouldn't know or understand the horror of what happened to me. I would wish for *someone—anyone—* to understand. That didn't happen because it is difficult. Fortunately, I did have a lot of good family and friends for support.

I tried not to feel sorry for myself, but I did. Why me? Why did this happen? I knew I couldn't do that, though. I knew I had to find a way to be strong. Having a stroke is like restarting your entire life, even if you don't want to. You have no choice.

This is my story. The events that led up to the brain trauma, the events in the hospital and rehabilitation hospitals, the physical therapy, divorce, and especially all the people along the way who helped me, encouraged me, and stood by me.

There is a lot to learn when you go through such a tremendously life-altering trauma. Mostly, I felt unheard, misunderstood, and hopeless to change it. I hope my story can help those who go through similar traumas, but especially their families and friends.

Since I remembered very little for a year, I have relied on notes taken by my wife at the time, and recollections of others for those passages. Thank you to the hospital staff, medical professionals, physical therapists, friends, coworkers family, and many others, but especially my children, Alexa and Logan, who have helped me far more than they know.

Every so often I look at my life today, and I cannot believe what it is like. No one could've predicted it, least of all me. I look around and say, "how did I get here?!" This most often happens if I see some of my post stroke pictures and videos. I looked so frail and dependent. I needed help to just get through a morning. I had gone from what I thought was a cool, strong, independent man, to a needy, insufficient mess. Such an extreme is such a hard pill to swallow. One cannot just "roll with it" or brush it off. When cannot just forget it and move ahead.

On the other hand, as I have said many times, the personal growth that comes is incredible. Scary? Yes. Overwhelming at times? Yes. But not without purpose and meaning.

Life will throw us curves, and this is what makes good times special. Not always knowing what is ahead keeps one on their toes. I've always said that I would much rather ride a roller coaster than a merry-go-round in life. I laugh when I say that I should have been careful what I wished for because I certainly got the roller coaster!

There is no instruction manual or book that can teach you how to handle overwhelming obstacles, even though there are many resources that can help. I know I must evolve and play the hand I was dealt. I'm not a Pollyanna, this has been extremely hard, more so that I can even explain. And it continues to be difficult: I still have a lot of work to do. No, I still need to work on being more patient and less judgmental of others. I need to offer them grace and be kind, for most of them have never walked in my shoes.

I had to learn to accept that this is the life I'm supposed to live. It wasn't what I planned on, but we are all dealt a hand in life: we may not like it, but our only choice is to adapt or give up. Someone once said that, "in the midst of suffering and obstacles, we can choose to get better or to get bitter." I choose to fight and do my best to grow, to a better person, and to enjoy the blessings in my life. I'm getting there, despite the setbacks and ups and downs.

This is my story.

Dan with his children before the accident

The Call to my Wife

"Hello?"

Why would her husband's chiropractor be calling her on her cell phone at work?

"Staci, this is Shahira at the chiropractor's office."

"Hi, Shahira." Maybe Dan missed his appointment. But why would—

"Dr. Jensen was adjusting Dan, and he went unconscious."

"What happened? Is he okay?" It felt like her heart stopped, and she couldn't move.

"I don't know, the ambulance is on its way."

Staci jumped up from her desk, fished her keys out of her purse, and headed out of the office, still holding the cell phone to her ear. "I'm on my way! Should I come there or to the hospital?"

"Go to St. John's."

She reached her car and fumbled with the keys, swearing at her shaking hands. She got in and turned on the car, and then realized that the kids were home alone. *What do I do?*

One on her way, she called Aimee, a close and longtime family friend. She explained that something that happened to me at the chiropractor and that I was on my way to the hospital. Could Aimee go get the kids? Aimee said she would be happy to. She asked what she should say to them. Staci asked her not to tell them anything, just that she had to run an errand. Amy said she would just tell them that Dan's doctor appointment was running late.

She breathed a sigh and called Shahira back.

"What's going on?"

"I… I don't know…I…" She sounded as if she were in shock, which did not make Staci feel any better. "Shahira! What's happening? Is the ambulance there?"

"No. Yes. Yes…and the firemen."

"Fireman? Why?"

"I—" there was commotion in the background and sounded like someone was asking Shahira something, and Shakira responded off-phone.

"Shahira! Let me talk to one of the ambulance people."

She heard her ask, but didn't hear the reply. "They won't—they can't talk right now."

Staci felt like her head would explode. *What was going on?* "Let me talk to one of the firemen!"

There was more commotion and talking, and then a man's voice was on the phone. "Is this Dan's wife?"

"Yes! Yes, this is Staci. What's going on with Dan?"

"Where are you right now?"

"I'm driving! What's going on with Dan?!"

"OK, good. You need to drive to Saint John's Hospital in Oxnard. You know where that is, right? Your husband was getting a treatment and something went wrong, and he is not doing well, but they are taking care of him. He's in the ambulance on his way. Do you understand? St. Johns."

Her heart was in her throat. "Yes, yes. On my way." She hung up and choked back a sob. *Why is this happening? Why is this happening?*

Her mind was both numb and racing at the same time, she was at the emergency entrance at St. John's Hospital before she knew it, having no memory of the drive. She parked and ran inside.

"I'm Staci, Dan's wife. Is he here yet? What is going on?"

The nurse behind the counter didn't even look up the info. "He is being taken care of. Once they are settled, they will let you back. Have a seat."

How can I sit still?! She sat anyway, then got up and paced. Then sat again. It seemed like an eternity before she saw a firefighter and an ambulance driver come through the doors to the back. She jumped up. "Excuse me, did you just transport Dan McSkimming here?"

The firefighter answered. "Yes, yes, they are taking care of him."

"What is going on? What is happening?"

"I don't really know, ma'am. Something happened during the chiropractic session. They are prepping him to be lifted to Santa Barbara."

"What? Why? What's wrong with him?"

"Honestly, ma'am, I don't know, but he was stable—"

"Staci?" A voice behind her. She turned and saw Chris, along with Brad, Eric, and the police and fire chaplain. People she knew! Chris was new to the SWAT team, a natural leader and intelligent. We called him "CG." Brad was a friend and fellow officer.

The momentary comfort was replaced by panic. *Why were all these people from Dan's work here? Why the chaplain?!*

She must have looked unsteady because Chris gently took her by the shoulders and set her in a chair. She started crying. They all gathered around, hands on her shoulders.

"It's okay, Staci, we're all here for support and anything you need. Dan's in good hands, and once stabilized, they will transport him to Cottage Hospital in Santa Barbara—the best in the area."

"How—is he going to be okay?"

He grimaced. "I don't know—all we know is that he is being taken good care of. They know he's a Deputy Sheriff, and they know all about him."

She wiped her eyes. "How?"

"Someone in the department is friends with Dr. Orr—the office called and told him about Dan, so he notified the agency. Everyone in the department is ready and prepared to help however we can."

Despite not knowing anything, It *was* a comfort. The police force that Dan worked with loved him, and were quality people.

What had happened at the doctor's office?!

The Injury at the Chiropractor

I was at work on patrol in Montecito, a county area just north of Carpinteria. Montecito is a beautiful little California seaside town—quaint and friendly. It lies just south of Santa Barbara and is about 84 miles (ca. 135 km) north of Los Angeles.

I had a rifle and a pistol with me. The rifle was a Smith & Wesson 40 caliber. I also had an HK Duty pistol. It was a .40 caliber, USP, set-automatic, blue-steel color. Its serial number was 22-22669. I had carried that pistol for twenty years, used it on patrol and during SWAT missions. I was attached to it—silly, maybe, but it had been with me throughout the course of my career. Shooting was never one of my favorite activities, but this was a great tool that I respected and appreciated.

Though I had not had the rifle as long as my pistol, I had adjusted and cleaned it many times. Sadly, the pistol disappeared, and no one had been able to find it.

Sitting in the driver's seat of my patrol car, I noticed that the rifle, to the right of me on its gun rack, was rattling as I drove. It was rattling in its gun lock. I pulled over into a nearby school parking lot to adjust it. In making this small movement, I tweaked my neck, causing an injury which led me to the Chiropractor's office. I felt a sharp and intense pain on the right side of my neck. I held steady, blinking with pain, and waited for it to go away. It did not. If I held my head straight, it was bearable, but turning my head in either direction at all was too painful.

Embarrassed, I drove back to the station and reported what happened to my Sergeant. He told me to take the day off and rest. I did so, and it was a little better, but not much. Back at home, I had tried everything for the pain heat, ice, massage, ibuprofen, stretching, but nothing worked. I had no idea what could have happened, but I knew I could not do my job in this condition.

I had been to Dr. Jensen, a chiropractor, a few times in the past for some minor back pain. So, I scheduled an appointment to see if he could relieve the pain in my neck. He examined me on that first visit, but said that there was some swelling, and he would rather not do any procedures until it abated. He suggested I come back the next day. I scheduled a second appointment and headed back home.

Little did any of us know how that small act would affect the rest of my life.

*

The next day, I was at home that afternoon with my son and daughter, 7 and 11 years old. I had cleaned up the kitchen, but left dishes in the sink to wash when I got back from my appointment. Staci was at work. I told the kids I was going to a chiropractor appointment, and I would be back in thirty minutes or so.

Our entire lives were about to be turned upside down.

At the office, I checked in and was soon with the chiropractor. We discussed the injury and my symptoms, and then he said he thought that adjusting my back would help. I arranged myself on the examination table as he suggested, he moved my limbs around a bit and then began adjusting. He then moved to my neck and did an adjustment.

It was the last thing I remembered clearly for a while, for a long time.

The paramedics arrived and immediately did what they could and prepared me for transport to St. John's Medical Center in Oxnard, about twenty minutes away. At some point, I woke up, and knew something was terribly wrong. I passed out again and did not remember anything for weeks.

The doctor was friends with someone in the police department, and he notified him about what happened and where I was going. The officer, in turn, alerted the department, and a number of my fellow officers and others headed there immediately. Then Shahira called Staci and told her what had happened.

I do not remember the trip to the hospital.

My Life

The journey of our lives often celebrate being born and then our death. But the middle is the most interesting part, of course. We sometimes think we can plan what happens to us, but typically, we have no choice but to adapt.

I was born on July 6, 1971, in Santa Barbara. Ironically, I was born at Cottage Hospital, the place where I would end up as an adult, spending a couple of months during the worst trauma of my life.

My parents were David McSkimming and Anne Reuser. My dad worked for a cable television company and my mom was a bookkeeper. I have one sister, Elizabeth, who is four years older than me.

I grew up in Santa Barbara. I recall life being like an adventure. One of my standout memories is riding around on my big wheel tricycle. I was curious about everything going on around me, and I was always getting into mischief.

I attended public schools and played sports—nothing particularly unusual or outstanding. I went to Santa Rosa Junior College. I decided that I wanted to study criminal justice, so I transferred to Sonoma State University for my degree.

Once I had my degree, I was selected to do an internship with the federal probation office in San Francisco. It taught me that I wasn't as interested in federal law-enforcement as I was local law enforcement. My first job after the internship was working on loss prevention at the juvenile hall in Santa Rosa for Sonoma County. I often worked at night at a boys' probation camp as well. I remember once, while there, I fell asleep during the night while I was supposed to be working. My partner had fallen asleep as well, and we both woke up to a resident right in our faces. Fortunately, nothing happened because of this lapse. Lessons learned. I enjoyed my work tremendously, and it was so a great experience.

Eventually, I moved back to Santa Barbara and got a job at the boys' camp and juvenile hall in the county probation office. I also worked in downtown Santa Barbara at Nordstrom's in their loss prevention department, which was an intriguing job. They offered me a job in management in the same department at the Seattle store. But at that point, I had decided I wanted to attend the police academy. (interestingly, one of my coworkers at Nordstrom also went through the Academy with me, and now works at the Ventura County Sheriffs Office as a patrol sergeant. My boss at Nordstrom's became an excellent Deputy District Attorney for Santa Barbara County.

During that time, I married my college sweetheart, Sarah. We met at work in a group home, where we worked together as youth counselors. I had worked there for several months when she started. I walked into the office one day to collect my paycheck. She was there, training, with my boss, and she was talking. I cut her off and asked for my paycheck from my boss. She called me "a little rascal" for my interruption. It made an impression on me, and we started spending time together, started dating, and eventually were engaged and married. But we found we had different ideas and options about life. We grew apart, and decided it was best to separate and divorce. We were married less than a year. Sarah is a good person, and we are still friends.

I was married again five years later to a wonderful woman named Staci. We met in Santa Barbara while she was working at a restaurant that I visited with friends. We got it off and found out that we had friends in common. At that time, I lived in Santa Barbara, and she lived in Camarillo, about 45 miles (ca. 72 km) apart. We made time for each other by making the drive between the two towns. The geographic distance didn't make a difference to us at the time: we were young, passionate, and in love.

We lived in Santa Barbara for a couple of years, then decided to move to Camarillo, get married, and start a family. We had a remarkable son in 2002, who we named Logan. In 2007, we welcomed an equally remarkable daughter, Alexa.

I continued working in Santa Barbara. We bought a house in a nice housing tract, and were living a typical and enjoyable life as a young family.

We had no idea what was ahead.

*

I could have chosen a different career. I was accepted into law school, but I wanted a more active career and I would rather not keep sitting in classrooms. I don't regret my decision despite my injury—being an officer was fun, challenging, and rewarding.

A few events stand out in my mind about my time at the academy. I remember the first day. Despite all my preparations, I was nervous and scared as hell. I had participated in a Pre-Academy course, but I was uncertain if I was ready for the Academy. It was also my 27th birthday. I remember that day that decided not to say anything to anyone—that's my style, anyway. However, in this "boot-camp" style environment, I thought it was best to draw little attention.

I was scared as hell, and not sure that I was ready for this.

The Tactical Officers (Tac's) marched in, looking severe and professional. They called on us individually, and told his to stand and answer a few questions: our name, the department we were with, and any previous law enforcement experience that you brought with you.

I noticed a couple of cute girls in my class. One hot day, we were ordered to go on a long run. One of the girls got heat stroke, and the staff told us to grab a nearby water hose and "hose her down." Unfortunately, we were wearing our standard issue white t-shirts, so it was like a wet t-shirt contest. She had to be embarrassed, yet no one said a word, even though surely they all noticed. We were all cadets in this together.

During the academy, the Department paid for us to live in an apartment. While the physical training was good, I wanted more, so I joined a local gym.

One training day was called "The Will to Survive." The Tac's matched each of us with another cadet who was a similar in size and frame. They strapped boxing gloves on us and told us to go at it for two or three minute rounds.

The powers-that-be appointed one of us to be the Class Corporal. It was a great honor, but at the same time, they got a lot of crap from the Tac's. I knew it was a test—like boot camp—to see if we had what it takes. Occasionally, an appointed class corporal could not handle the pressure and failed, and they were terminated from the program. Fortunately for me, I was not appointed until near the end of the program. By that time, I knew what it took, and I was able to handle it.

*

Although a career in law enforcement is a wonderful experience, an officer never forgets his or her academy training. We move to Filed Training and then onto probation, but the experience with the academy staff and fellow cadets is timeless. I will never forget the camaraderie, the struggles, the joys, and the time they put us through the "Scary Dairy" (an old, abandoned building). It's a complex building, like a maze, with unpredictable doorways and hallways, especially difficult to navigate it once filled with smoke from the gas that was pumped in from tanks. The purpose of this was for us to experience exposure to different gasses, such as CS (chlorobenzylidene malononitrile, a type of nerve gas) and pepper spray, which are the most commonly used riot control agents. As for the pepper spray, we were exposed to it by being sprayed in the face by the Tech Officers at the academy facility. Pepper spray is commonly used and carried by police officers on their "Sam Browne belt," which we call a duty belt, worn around the waist. Today, police use utility vests to avoid hip problems to better balance the weight of the equipment.

Field training was stressful for me, but I learned a lot. As a youngster, I had been taught to "mind my own business." But part of a police officer's job is to get involved in a stranger's "business." As officers, we are often seeing people at the worst or at their lowest point. Many are distressed and looking for answers and help. It is important how we act in those situations because those people we interact with will always remember how they were treated (fairly or unfairly).

From the academy, I embarked on an 18-year career as a police officer: Sixteen years on the streets and 18 years total in the official books (where the county recorded such information). This included 13 years on the SWAT team, which I served simultaneously as a collateral assignment. I enjoyed it and my co-workers, who are some of the best people I have ever met. More than that, it is our job, and we are trained to do it the best we can. It's been popular in recent times to criticize law enforcement because of some failures. In my experience, it is not a systematic problem. That's not to say there's a need for some reforms in some areas (which is true of any large and old organization). Everyone that I met went out each day ready to lay their lives on the line for fellow citizens, without any concern for appreciation or thanks. It's our job, and we are trying to do the best we can.

Ten years after my Academy training, I was a Tactical Officer at that same Police Academy, where I trained five classes along with other talented TACs. This was a great experience to be on the other side. A career in law enforcement is fulfilling, and even with required ongoing field training and work probation, an officer never forgets his Academy experience. The camaraderie, fear, frustration, the difficult days, and the bonding that takes place, is unique.

As TACs, we often had to make quick uniform changes. One of my coworkers' locker was right next to mine, and every so often he would just start stripping down. Every time, I would shout, "Hey, warn a brother!" It became a running joke among all of us. To this day, it still makes me laugh to think about it.

When my accident happened, and I retired, I was a Senior Deputy on patrol in the City of Carpinteria and the County of Montecito. I trained with my SWAT team twice a month as a collateral assignment.

*

There is a difference between being hired as an employee of a government and being hired in the private sector. Government agencies typically require background checks and a polygraph test. If you pass those, there is then an oral exam for placement and possibly being hiring. In the private sector, it is usually just a series of interviews, which can sometimes be intensive depending on the position.

I hated the process, but I understand its importance. We want those who patrol our streets in our society to be under scrutiny—we want them to be the best. In my experience, as I wrote above, most officers fit these descriptions. But inadequate people still slip through the process sometimes and become law enforcement officers. I saw this during my training, when I was teaching, and talking to friends who were assigned to HR and performing background investigation. The people in charge of the hiring process are human, and mistakes can be made, records can be missed, and a candidate may not be forthcoming. He or she can even change over time while on the job. There is no perfect system, but most officers are good people and work hard. Unfortunately, like in all professions, bad hiring happens occasionally. And even though there aren't very many bad ones, those are the ones that stand out when they make terrible mistakes because we are in the public eye.

*

Most people don't know the difference between a Police Department and Sheriff's Department. The primary difference is the areas in which they work. Police patrol the incorporated areas and the cities, whereas Sheriffs patrol the unincorporated areas of the county. Sometimes, cities will contract with a Sheriff's Department to provide public safety or other police services so that they can obtain more services for less money and not have to develop their own police department. That's why, in some cities, you see "Sheriff" on the back of the car and "City Police" on the side. Occasionally, the city name will be displayed as well.

There are other minor differences. Sheriffs are elected, but the city appoints police chiefs. The Sheriff's Office usually provides jails, and security at courthouses. Cities and Counties often have their own Tactical Team or SWAT Teams. But of course, both police and sheriffs work together constantly.

*

Many stories and cases stand out as I think back on my career. I remember one SWAT team training exercise in particular. It was a night training session, and involved swimming in the ocean. We were to jump out of a helicopter into the sea, then swim to a Sheriff's boat.

When it came to my turn to jump (carefully timed between the man before me and the man after me), I noticed the man before me had not hit the water yet—we were too high! I hit the ocean, and it felt like smacking into concrete. One of our teammates passed out when he hit the water, resulting in a couple of cracked ribs. I was mad at the pilot, but we were lucky things were not worse. I had bruises on my legs and glutes, a small price to pay for a good lesson.

*

I don't often discuss cases that I worked on, but I'll mention a few that stood out during my career. Some of the cases I dealt with were big cases, and many were very difficult emotionally and mentally. Little did I know that the hardest challenge I would face was just ahead in my life.

*

I worked on the Jesse James Hollywood case in 2000. Jesse Hollywood was a drug dealer who kidnapped Nicholas Markowitz, a half brother of Ben Markowitz, who owed Hollywood $1,200 for marijuana. Hoping to use Nicholas as leverage over his brother's head, Hollywood got concerned when someone told him that kidnapping could bring a life sentence. So, he supplied a gun to an associate to murder him.

A friend of mine was working on mountain patrol when Nicholas Markowitz' body was found in a shallow grave in the hills above Santa Barbara, California. I was called in to secure the scene. Of course, the detectives had already removed the body, but the scene had to still be processed by the Forensics Unit and therefore needed to be protected. Being a young deputy. I was the one tapped for securing the scene overnight. Alone, in the mountains, at the site of a grisly scene, is something that will always stick in my mind—all the more so because it was a high-profile case. Hollywood was eventually arrested and is serving a life sentence without parole. (A movie was made about the murder, entitled *Alpha Dog*.)

Years later, I was a Supervisor on the Gang Unit and assigned to transport and trial security for Hollywood's murder trial. Many authorities were concerned that Hollywood's father might somehow help him escape justice. I made sure nothing went wrong. I had great training from the Special Enforcement Team SET (SWAT). I picked him up from the jail each morning during the trial, making sure he was dressed and secure for the trial. I often accompanied him during the lunch break. Near the end of the trial, as we transported Hollywood back to jail, he asked me if I thought he should have testified on his own behalf. His legal team—flashy, likable, high-profile Los Angeles defense attorneys—had told him that he should not. I knew he wanted to testify, but I also knew this was a defendant that just did not get it. He was more concerned about the reviews for *Alpha Dog* than the possibility of spending life in prison. I informed him that, in my opinion, it would be a mistake for him to take the stand on his own behalf. I found him to be a likable man, but he ruined his life by killing someone over a relatively small marijuana debt. As an officer, we were not supposed to voice our opinions, but today I can say that he deserved what he got.

*

The second case that always sticks in my mind was the Michael Jackson trial. Of course, we are all aware of the talent of Michael Jackson. In 2005, in Santa Maria,

California, I was part of the security team and crowd control for protesters and aggressive fans outside the courthouse during his hearing. Michael Jackson owned Neverland Ranch in Santa Maria—a vast property that he upgraded extensively and changed to his taste. Years later, the property was sold to a private company, my SET team organized some training activities with the residential security at Neverland. I spent some time at Neverland and inside the massive mansion. CCTV monitors were everywhere. The clothing in his closets was meticulously labelled. There were deadbolts on his bedroom door, and a passageway between his room and the kitchen, so his staff could deliver food and drinks. There was also a stairway between his room and the rooms where kids would stay. A theater was part of the property as well, with a carpeted room beneath the stage. It all looked fishy to me, and so many had come forward to accuse him. But I was not privy to all the evidence against and for him. Every person can judge what they think, of course.

*

Once, a criminal complaint came in from Oprah Winfrey's house in Montecito, California. I was assigned to go out and take the report. I met with Oprah's trainer and house manager. They told me that Oprah had written a book, and her house manager, Mr. Green, been in Chicago promoting it. An obsessed woman began stalking him, even when he returned to California, and began doing the same to Opra's trainer. Most of it was through emails, which were relentless.

I met with an employee in one of the houses on the property. As I was asking questions, and he was telling me what happened, I kept hearing a strange pounding and a motor running. I asked what it was, and he replied, "Oprah is on the treadmill around the corner. I can ask her to stop if you wish." I told him not to interrupt her, I just wondered what it was.

He then finished telling me what the stalker had been doing, and showed me copies of several emails that she kept sending. I knew that the case would be taken over by the detectives in Chicago, since that's where the woman was from. They had jurisdiction, so my role was to forward my report to the Chicago Police Department.

The manager was a very nice person and gave me all the information I needed. At the end, I mentioned that I would like to meet Oprah. He said, "Not while she's working out." I told him that I understood that, and I left. I did not get to meet Oprah, though I did get to see her beautiful property.

*

The final case I recall had a big effect on me in my career. Three young people had decided to go to a party in Montecito. As they were leaving, two of the girls, who were drunk, decided to try "car surfing." This is where you stand on the trunk, roof, or hood—like a surfboard—while the car is being driven. As the car went over a bridge, going way too fast, it hit a bump and the girls flew off and one was seriously injured. The other two put her in the car and drove to the hospital. It was too late. She did not survive.

The other girl who survived was the daughter of a high-ranking CHP officer in Santa Barbara, and she wanted to avoid revealing that they were drunk and car surfing. I was in the hospital with her father as she told him about the incident, omitting important details. I knew she was lying, based on the scene. It was difficult for me to listen to her try to cover for her and her friend who was driving. I understood why she was doing it, but a young girl was dead. She only made matters worse by lying about what happened.

The detectives in the tow company at the scene were trying to be professional, but they made the situation worse. Because the girl wasn't forthcoming, the circumstance of the death was not clear. When the detectives saw all the decease's blood inside the vehicle, the car should have been towed and stored for observation because a possible crime might have occurred. But we didn't know the full story, so there was still a need for more investigation.

When I returned to the station, I showed some pictures of the scene to one of the detectives, who noticed a scrape on the hood of the vehicle. It was later determined that that scrape was a rub mark from the girl's heel as she flew off the car.

She finally admitted the truth about the circumstances of the accident and death. She was trying to protect the drunk driver, but the truth was going to come out eventually. She only made things worse for the families and the officers by not being truthful from the beginning.

This was a terrible accident that came about through the reckless behavior of young people. Knowing what actually happened didn't make it any easier. This was a difficult case and scene that affects me to this day.

*

Dealing with these (and more) horrific cases had an impact on me, of course. I dealt with plenty of gruesome things, but certain events influence a person more than others. Anyone who says these kinds of things don't bother them is not being honest. While I had a tendency, like many in my situation, to "brush things off" and just keep going, these things build up in your mind. I didn't have all the answers, but I learned that if you don't deal with the psychological effects of witnessing trauma, they will come back to bite you eventually. Police officers are humans, not machines. They experience anxiety, and post-traumatic stress syndrome, just like other people. We do our best, but we're not superhuman.

As I wrote above, I could have selected a different profession. I would rather not be in school for a long time. I wanted to be active and not sedentary. I don't regret my career choice, but at times it was challenging, to say the least. I may have chosen the hard road, but that's okay because I love helping people in time of need. Being a Deputy Sheriff was rewarding and made me feel like I had a purpose. A stroke, a divorce, early retirement—difficult, yes, but I would not change any of it, even if I could.

Emergency Room and Cottage Hospital — August

Eventually, they let Staci in to see me, and began asking her many questions about me, especially my health and why I was at a chiropractor. She answered as best she could. While still worried, at least she was with me and involved in the care.

The doctors contacted a specialist in Sacramento, who reviewed me and my case remotely, looking over my MRI, CT scan, and all the other tests they had performed. He concluded that I had had a blood clot in one of my arteries in my neck. This sometimes happens, and they usually dissolve over time and heal themselves without the person even knowing they had it. When Dr. Jensen adjusted my neck, it released the blood clot, which travelled to my brain and caused a massive stroke. Specially, he determined it was an "Ischemic Stroke," which affects most motor skills. It is not medically treatable. He suggested I should be moved to Santa Barbara Cottage Hospital, which had specialists on site for just such conditions.

The staff decided that time was of the essence, and that I should be airlifted to Cottage. Brad and the Fire Battalion Chief, Chris, told Staci that they were available to help support whatever was needed to help. Dr. Jensen also showed up to follow my progress.

I do not remember any of this because I was still unconscious. Later, Staci shared with me that the doctors and staff all commented on my excellent physical shape, saying I looked like a "buff Ken doll" as they had trouble getting the blood pressure cuff around my biceps.

They prepped me for travel via helicopter. I do not remember the trip, though I have a faint memory of some strange dreams: I was in a helicopter and the pilots were strange, and we were running out of fuel. When the helicopter landed, the flight nurses took over preparation with skill and care.

Staci left the hospital to drive to Santa Barbara, about a 30-minute trip. Dr. Jensen, worried about me, said he was going to follow her to Cottage Hospital. Staci remembered that my truck was at his office, and asked him about it. He asked her to give him the keys, and he would make sure it got back to our house.

*

At that time, my mother and my sister got calls on both of their phones. They were driving on the 101 freeway, just about an hour north of me, near Santa Barbara, with my niece and nephew.

They were all in shock when they heard the news. They quickly changed their route to go to Cottage Hospital. As they drove, they saw the helicopter go by overhead—with me in it, flying north over the ocean.

They arrived before I was even in my room, asking what happened. The nurse was kind enough to tell them that I had a stroke. My sister began to cry.

*

The helicopter landed, and my SWAT team was waiting outside. They saluted me as I was taken into the hospital. Others began arriving at the hospital, but I was aware of it. I only learned of the events, and the comings and goings of people, through the notes that Staci took.

Along with many of my fellow officers and staff, my mom and sister arrived at the hospital that day. They hugged Staci and spoke with her, then set to work trying to plan arrangements for everyone who had shown up and who might show up later. Someone suggested to Staci that she needed to appoint someone to be a spokesperson, so she didn't have to deal with all the questions and updates for people. She chose Tony and Steve. I had worked with Tony for some time—he was also on the SWAT team after me. Everyone called him, "The Greek." Steve was also on the SWAT team, though not at the same time as me. We called him "Gonzo," and he is quite a good guy. His father was the Chief of Police in Santa Paula, and had recently passed away in 2022. Steve was so helpful to me during my time dealing with the accident. Both "The Greek" and "Gonzo" are good friends to this day.

Staci and others were led to a waiting room outside the room where the doctors would perform several procedures on me. Dr. Zoner was assigned to me, and he told Staci about the procedures. Later, Staci said it all seemed like a dream—she was just listening and going through the motions, almost like a robot.

Soon, they rolled me by on a gurney. When they reached Staci, she took my hand and squeezed it, and gave me a kiss. She said, "I love you," before they wheeled me away. It's nice to know I had so much support, but of course, I don't remember any of it.

The number of people in the waiting room was overwhelming to Staci. She said it was like the President was in the operating room. She was beginning to be overwhelmed by the number of phone calls and text messages coming in, as word began to spread about what had happened to me and the seriousness of it.

Eventually, I came out of the operating room and into the ICU. I was put in a big, pleasant corner room with a delightful view of the walking grounds. Staci was allowed in after a while, and the nurses introduced themselves to her.

Many of my co-workers were there in the waiting room, for support, even though they knew they would not be getting in to see me anytime soon.

A few of my closest friends, Doug, Steve, Tony, Eric, Brad, Sandy, and Marc, were in the waiting room, along with many others, wanting to show their support event though they knew they would not be allowed to see me any time soon. Just knowing that they were there gave Staci peace of mind. Doug was on the SWAT team with me. He is such a hard worker and a good family man. Sandy was always good to me—he was also on the SWAT team with me before his promotion. He's a good teacher, dad, and officer. Marc became one of my best friends and confidents. We'd been through a lot of training together. I remember when he made it on SET. He's been through a lot himself, but was so supportive of me.

They set up a schedule so that someone would always be there, and to give Staci a break if she needed it. Chris and Sandy took the first shift—Sandy even went and got a sleeping bag! Staci was so touched by their willingness to be present when they were off the clock, just to provide support and encouragement.

Staci's mom arrived in Camarillo from Temecula, about a three-hour drive, to take care of the kids at our house. She called Staci so that they could talk to their mom. They asked her where I was and what had happened. At this point, Staci was not sure how much to tell them, or how bad it was. She said, "Dad hurt his neck and the doctors are fixing it. He'll stay at the hospital until he is healed." Alexa asked, "Did it break off?" Staci was able to laugh and say, "No, his head did not break off. He will be fine."

She decided to stay the night with me. She found a jacket in the trunk and a nurse gave her some warm socks. That night was a tough one, so I was told. I was quite restless, and would not have gotten much sleep anyway, as the nurses came in and out to take my blood pressure, do checks on my balance, and assess the movement of my extremities. At some point during the night, I apparently yelled out, causing Staci to jump out of her chair and the nurses to come running.

They were working to get my fever down by giving me a cold bath, and when that didn't work, the nurses packed ice bags on my side and cranked up the air conditioner. My blood pressure was also quite high. Both the fever and blood pressure was caused by the swelling in my brain. Around 3:30am, they gave me morphine, and I slept.

They got me up at 5:00am on Wednesday, August 13, for a CT scan, rolling me out and into the CT room. Since it would take about 30 minutes, Staci went to check on all the guys who were still in the waiting room. Eric was coming at 7am to relieve them.

When they brought me back into the room, I was quite lethargic. Around 8:30am, Dr. Zoner came in with a team of what seemed liked twenty people (according to Staci). After examining me, he told Staci that there was still a lot of swelling. Once more, he went over the procedure and other updates with her.

Staci decided that she would run home for a shower and to pack a bag. On her way back, Dr. Zoner called.

"Staci, since Dan is alert and restless because of the fever and blood pressure reading. His body does not have the resources to heal. I think the best bet now is to put him into a medically induced coma."

Her heart sank.

Learning to Live After the Trauma of a Stroke

*

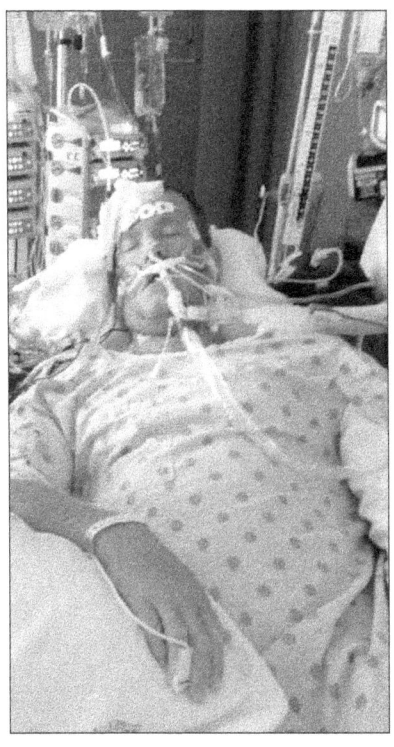

Of course, I was not aware of this, and did not know until much later that I was in an induced coma for two weeks.

When Staci arrived at the hospital, they already had me sedated and were preparing to put a breathing tube down my throat. She had to wait outside while they did the procedure, not even getting to see me before I went into the medically induced coma.

Finally allowed inside, Staci said later that she watched me lay in bed, with all those machines surrounding me: breathing for me, keeping my body temperature proper, monitoring my blood pressure and the brain pressure. She just wanted to see me turn my head and say hi to her. She thought about the kids, who kept asking about their dad, but all she could say was that he hurt his neck and the doctors were working on him. Though she knew, at some point, she was going to have to tell them more, watching me lay in bed helpless, she could not bring herself to do it.

It did make her feel better that the hospital had assigned a nurse just to me, who rarely even left the room.

*

Much later, I asked my daughter to write a little of what she felt on that day. She wrote the following:

When I was only 5-years-old at 12:00 in the afternoon and my Dad had told me and my ten-year-old brother, Logan, was going to watch me for an hour while he was at the Chiro-Tractor's. Dad left the house and drove away, hours flew by like a jet, and he still wasn't home. We got a call from my Mom, she called to tell us we were going to her friend Ami's house and that our Grandma would pick us up there in about two hours. Me and my brother got there and didn't know what was going on. When my Grandma got there, we asked what was going on and why Dad was not home yet. She told us that our Dad had been air lifted to the hospital and that he had a Stroke and could possibly die, and that we needed to pray that he was going to live. When she told me I hadn't known what that was but when I heard the five words "hospital" and "hope he is okay" I knew something was wrong and the feeling that I had felt like someone just threw a 100-mph-bolder at my heart and stomach. When we headed back to the house, we felt like we were going to cry like our tears were "Niagara Falls" and that we weren't going to see our Dad ever again.

*

The next day, Thursday, Staci went to check on the guys who were taking shifts in the waiting room. They have all said that they wanted to be here for her and I. At one point, while the nurses were making a shift change, Staci went out to visit Doug. He had worked all night on a SWAT call out, but was now here taking his shift. She felt so sorry for him. She talked to Steve and let him know that she appreciated them more than she could express, but she felt bad for them holding these vigils. Furthermore, she said, maybe it would be better when he's awake and looking for conversation and company. Steve, the one who had arranged it all, said that he understood, and he would pass the message along.

Later that day, they took me down for another CT scan. Dr. Zoner decided that I needed a feeding tube in order to get more calories in me. Yes, another tube running into my body.

Staci spent much of the day standing by my bedside, rubbing my arm, kissing my head, and hoping that in some way, I could hear her and feel her. She thought to herself that this was the longest we had ever gone without talking since we'd met.

She was getting used to sleeping in the chair through the night.

*

Staci got into a routine by Friday, sleeping in the chair at night, brushing her teeth and changing clothes in the bathroom while the nurses did the morning shift change. Then she went to check on the guys who were still there.

One morning, when the guys were still there, she decided she could run home. She took a shower, watered the lawn, then prepared to head back. Doug called and said that he and Steve talked and decided they would tell the guys they didn't need to stay anymore for now. They would resume their shifts when they were needed in the future.

When she arrived back at the hospital, Chris and Tyler were waiting there to see her before they left. The staff allowed them both into the room to see me. Staci could see that they were visibly shaken when they saw my condition.

My Dad arrived and stayed in the room for a while, speaking with Staci. She said it was sweet to see him rubbing my foot as they talked. Later, Erik and Heather arrived in the waiting room. Erik used to be on the SWAT team with me, and Heather was a forensic tech I had worked with as a detective. They had brought bags of snacks, bottles of water, and other things, along with a Starbucks card and a gas card. Staci said it was too generous, but they insisted.

My Dad left and Staci was alone with me once more. She was trying to be strong, but as time went on, with all the unknowns, she felt like she was going to lose it.

She thought she should probably go home, but she really didn't want to leave me. Finally, at 9:30pm that night, she decided that she needed to go home. She kissed me good night, and told the nurse she'd call when she got home just to check on me.

At the house, she finds flowers from many supportive friends and family, along with wine and food, on the front doorstep. My close friend and coworker, Marc, called and asked if he could take her and the kids out to dinner Sunday night. Staci burst into tears. It was all hitting her now, and it came rushing out. She apologized to Marc, but of course, he understood.

That night, with the kids staying with her mom, Staci could not bring herself to sleep in our bed without me, so she slept on the couch.

*

On Saturday, a CT scan showed some fluid build-up in my lungs. The respiratory doctor had some concerns about my left lung—it seems quite full of fluid. So he set a schedule to remove more fluid more often.

Doug visited the hospital with pictures and emails, as well as some insurance paperwork he said he would help me with. Later, Staci told me that she was so impressed with how helpful and attentive my friends were —they overwhelmed her with their generosity, time, and willingness to do anything to help.

She invited Doug in to see me. When they entered the room, Doug was visibly choked up at the sight. As she stood by my side, rubbing my foot, Dr. Zoner came in, accompanied by a lung specialist and others. As they began to examine me and discuss my dire situation, Staci felt overwhelmed again. Her legs shook and her heart raced. She felt like she might pass out and had to sit down.

They decided to insert a scope down my throat into my right lung to take a look because they were afraid I might have aspirated and might be developing pneumonia.

Staci's mom and sister arrived, so Staci went back out into the waiting room to see them. My dad then showed up as well. Staci later told me it was strange seeing them together in the same room (they had divorced when I was about two years old).

Staci was so worried about our children because she had still not told them much. She also knew that they needed her presence. Until today, her mom had been with the kids, but she was bringing them home today. They had not asked many questions apart from how I was doing and when I was coming home. The hospital provided some professional pediatric counseling to Staci on how to talk to young children about such situations.

Staci decided it was time to give them more details about the situation. It broke her heart to think of telling them more, of course, but she knew she had to do it. She decided to leave me with the family members and go home.

The talk went well, as could be expected, but of course, they were upset and scared. Unsurprisingly, they want to see me. However, the nurse thought it would be best to have the child life specialist from the hospital present at the first visit, and she is not back to work until Monday.

That night, Staci called the hospital three times to check with the nurses. Each time, they told her I was doing well, which gave her a some relief and helped her to sleep better.

*

Tiffany, a family friend, took the kids to go spend the day with Tiffany's kids, Chase and Isabelle, which allowed Staci to come back and sit with me most of the day.

Marc wanted to take Staci and the kids out to dinner, so he came to the hospital. Staci asked if he wanted to see me, and he did. She told me later he choked up as he rubbed my arm and whispered to me. She was moved by his compassion.

Tiffany brought the kids to the lobby, and they all went to dinner with Marc. Staci said it was quite nice, but difficult for her to be away from me. Alexa took to Marc and thought he was young and cute! During the dinner, she told Marc, "I'm not going to call you 'dad'," which got a laugh from everyone. It was good to have some levity in the midst of this nightmare. They talked about me and told stories. Staci thought it was good for the kids.

Marc brought them back to the hospital and stayed with the kids, while Staci came up to see me briefly. She said goodnight and left with the kids for home. She said they were excited because they get to see me tomorrow.

*

Staci told me later that the kids woke up excited, nervous, and a little scared. Staci had shown them a picture of me in the hospital bed so that they would be prepared for what I looked like.

They drove to the hospital and met first with the Child Life Specialist, Vicky. Logan didn't like it, he just wanted to get in and see his dad!

Finally. They went to the room. Lex walked in and went immediately to the bedside and stood. Someone brought her a chair and she sat down. Logan held back for a bit, taking it all in. Then he walked slowly to the beside and touched my hand.

After a while, Logan asked to go to the bathroom, and as Staci walked him out, she could see he was a mess. She told him it was okay to cry or be mad or whatever he was feeling It was normal and sad, and she shared that she was mad sometimes and cried a lot. They sat for a while outside, talking, and then Logan said he was ready to go back in.

The kids sat by me, holding my hand, rubbing my feet, and asking countless questions. Staci thought that was a good sign.

Learning to Live After the Trauma of a Stroke

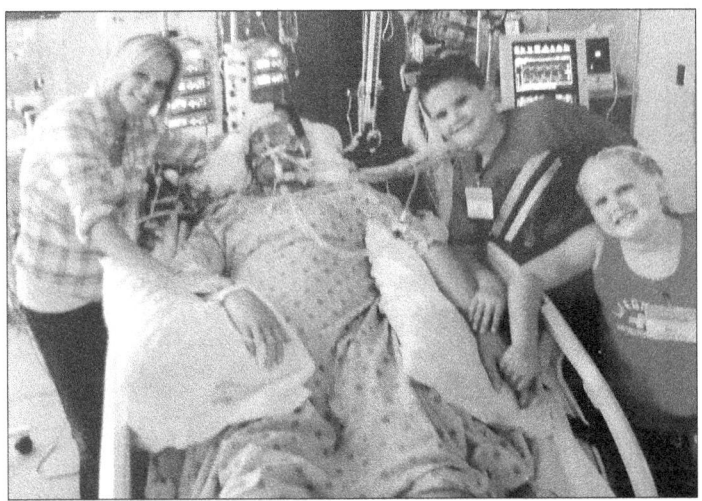

Later, they went down to the cafeteria. The kids were excited about all the options available, and said they couldn't wait to come down here with Dad once he woke up. Back in the room, they were both more comfortable, holding my hand and talking to me. Lexi read aloud a letter that she had written to me.

They left and went to a nearby shopping area to look for school backpacks. While there, Staci saw a See's Candy store, and asked the kids if they would like to buy candy for all the nurses attending to their dad. She told Lex and Logan how wonderful the staff had all been. Back at the hospital, the nurses were thankful for the gifts.

Back at the hospital, neither wanted to leave me, but Logan was satisfied when Staci took a picture of them with me at his request.

*

Almost a week into my stay at Cottage Hospital, and my CT scan was looking good. The swelling has not gotten any worse, although they were still having to drain fluid. The night nurse, Aaron, gave me a shave, and Staci said it made me look much better—but now I have a mustache!

Aimee kept the kids all day, so Staci was able to be with me until 6pm. She left to go grocery shopping and pick up the kids.

On Wednesday, Staci took Logan to his seventh grade orientation, after which they come to the hospital. She told me later that the kids were better today—all the wires, tubes, and machines didn't scare them any longer. They held my hand and talked to me for a while, then settled into chairs with their iPads.

After a couple of hours, they left to go shopping on State Street in Santa Barbara. Logan read about a backpack he really wants at a store there. They enjoyed the nice break to get out in the sunshine and do some normal things.

Back at the hospital, they met my mom and sister, who had arrived to see me. The relationship between Staci and my mom has not alway been good, but she is trying. My body has warmed up today—a good sign!

That night, Staci and the kids went to Tiffany's for dinner.

My first week in the hospital has ended.

Staci stayed with me after taking Lexi for soccer gear—she has her first practice tonight. Her mom took the kids again, so Staci could stay with me. My mom visited as well, along with Tony. Staci and my Mom argued about who could see me and when.

The next day, Staci was able to stay with me all day again. She sat in a chair pulled up next to my bed, holding my hand while reading a book. It was such a comfort to touch me, but she so wished I would squeeze her hand back and open my eyes, so she could look in them. Of course, I could not. I was unaware of anything going on while in the induced coma.

On Friday, Dr. Taylor came by while Staci was here to give her some updates. He mentioned the possibility of doing a tracheotomy, which he explained was normal for someone in my condition. Still, it made her almost sick to her stomach, and scared for me.

Marc came by to visit. Again, as before, it was emotional for him because he is such a kind and sensitive man. He helped Staci with the worker's comp issues. Doug also came by, and helped Staci get signed in to our Aflac account, so she could review the policy and coverage. Doug is also sensitive, and despite her concern for me, it warmed her heart again to see the care and the love those guys had for me.

On Saturday, my mom and sister came up to see me in the morning, it being my mom's birthday, so Staci took the morning off and came to see me in the afternoon, since they only allow two people in my room at a time. Staci told me later that she sometimes felt selfish because she wanted to avoid sharing the time in the room with anyone—she wanted to be there always.

Mark and Michelle (my brother- and sister-in-law) came for a visit as well, asking if there was anything they could do.

They took me off the paralytics, which was a good sign, albeit a minor one. By now, Staci was getting to know the nursing staff quite well, and told me they could not have been more helpful and compassionate.

On Sunday, the kids came to see me again with Stacy. Lex ran up to me, grabbed my hand, and started talking. Logan went to the other side and said, "Hey, dad." It broke Staci's heart.

I had not made a sound or moved in over two weeks, but on Monday I started coughing. Staci and Marc (who was visiting) jumped up in surprise. A nurse ran in, asking Staci and Marc to leave while she called for help. Staci was in the hall freaking out, not knowing what was happening. But soon, the nurse practitioner came out and explained that it was fine, they had cleared my lungs, and the tracheotomy would help with such episodes.

They scheduled the tracheotomy for Thursday at 11am, when they would also put a PEG (feeding tube) in me. The doctors and nurses told Staci these things will speed my recovering. It is still scary for her, of course.

On Wednesday, when Staci arrived, a nurse told her that I had opened my eyes a couple of times. She was so excited! First, she had to meet Gary from Aflac downstairs to fill out paperwork and arrange to get copies of my medical records. Part of the problem was that we had no power of attorney—we never even thought we'd need to this early in life. She learned that she might have to get a temporary conservatorship put in place, so she can act on my behalf.

On Thursday, the tracheotomy and PEG procedures took place. Staci was a nervous wreck while waiting. It went well, and she sat with me all afternoon after. Travis also came by to go over the long-term disability with her and help fill it all the forms.

The next day there was some bleeding from the tracheotomy, but they resolved it quickly. The next step was to wait for me to have a bowel movement, which would be another sign of off my progress and healing.

When Staci came to see me that day, my eyes were open. I have no recollection of that moment, and she said it was clear that I couldn't see her or respond to her touch, but she could see I was slightly more aware. I was still coughing a lot, but the doctors told her that also was a good sign!

Finally, (they tell me) I had a major bowel movement. An excellent sign of progress, but hearing it later, I felt sorry for the Spencer, the ER nurse on duty that day.

*

By Saturday, August 30, I was breathing largely on my own. During that night, they switched the settings to merely assisting me with breathing, rather than doing it for me, like they might do with someone who had sleep apnea. They told Staci that I was opening my eyes a lot, and I might have been responding to some of the nurses' words. They also told her there were a lot of bowel movement going on. I never thought people could get so exciting about that!

The next day, they extended my PEG deeper into my small intestine, to help with digestion. I was twitching a lot, but they said that is because of some of the medications I am on, and nothing to worry about. Staci began talking to me, unsure if I could hear her.

Progress!

Cottage Hospital (September)

On September 1, Staci and the kids arrived to find the doctors and nurses doing their rounds and checking on my status. They watched from the door as I moved my mouth, and saw that my eyes were open. The kids were excited to see me. The staff said it was okay to come in, so they ran over and started talking as usual. Logan had a giant smile on his face.

A nurse brought Alexa a step stool, so she could reach my face. She wanted to wipe off the tears that would run down my face. One of the nurses said, "She should be a nurse when she grows up!"

Staci, the kids, and the nurse began asking me to smile. About the third time, I did so. They were so excited! Even the nurses were cheering with tears in their eyes. Staci told me later that it was such a wonderful moment after so much fear, anxiety, and waiting.

The next day, I was not as responsive. Staci asked the nurses what was going on. They told her that it was normal to have alert days and not-so-alert days—nothing to worry about. That day was quiet as Staci and the kids sat beside me, holding my hands.

On Wednesday, September 3rd, I went into surgery to have a shunt put in. Although it was a routine surgery, Staci was a nervous wreck while waiting for them to bring me back to the room. She said sitting in that empty room was lonely and disturbing.

When they brought me back, they had shaved half of my head. It looked funny, and Staci wondered why they didn't just shave the whole head. She felt sorry for me. I didn't care, obviously. I was still quite unaware of anything going on.

The surgery had gone well. Staci stayed with me as I rested and recovered. I was silent and unmoving. The next day, however, when she walked in, she said I opened my eyes, and she could see the recognition in them. Her heart was filled with joy.

*

On Saturday, when Staci came in to see me after attending Alexa's soccer game, she said I looked at her again —but this time I squeezed her hand. Knowing that I loved massages, she took some lotion and massaged my arms, hands, legs, and feet.

Marc and Chris came to see me later that day. Staci could see that I was aware that they were here. She believed it gave me comfort as I began to come out of the coma.

The next day, however, when the kids came with her again, and I did not wake up. They were disappointed, but Staci repeated what the nurses had told her—it is normal to have a good day and then a day like this. Being even a little awake really tires out a patient like me as we heal.

The next day, I was wide awake and breathing 100% on my own. Tony and Greg came by, followed later by my Aunt Lori and Uncle Fred.

*

On Tuesday, September 9th, I had been in the hospital for a month. The doctors decided to see if I could respond to physical therapy. I did, although it tired me out quickly.

I began a period of being more tired and less alert. The doctors believed I was fighting an infection because I had a slight fever and my white cell blood count was high. They decided to try to sit me on the side of the bed—the first time I had sat up in a month! Staci watched and said her heart went out to me because the simple act of sitting was difficult. It took three of the staff to help me. They asked, "Do you feel dizzy?" and I nodded my head. They put me back down, and I immediately went to sleep.

Soon I was able to sit in a chair. Staci and the kids then noticed how much weight I had lost. One day, when Staci and Alexa were there, the staff wanted to check for seizures (perhaps because I was falling asleep so easily, and not able to be woken up.) They hooked up an EEG for 24 hours. This entailed about 30 or 40 pads on my head, each one glued down, with wires to the machine. Alexa didn't like it, so she found a bandage and wrapped it around my head to hide the sensors.

Finally, on Friday, Staci came to see me and there I was, wide awake. I was wide awake and began interacting with her. She was so excited!

On Saturday, they still suspected an infection, and believed it might be a bacterial infection, which they diagnosed as Clostridioides Difficile (CDiff). They placed my room on isolation, and Staci had to wear a hospital gown and gloves to get in to see me. While I had a fever and was a bit out of it, Staci and I watched about four hours of television together. A simple act, but so meaningful.

Despite the setbacks, I was making progress.

*

My infection was giving doctors some trouble. My CDiff count was headed past 30,000, which was far too high. They called in an infectious disease doctor, who examined me and surmised it might be a urinary tract infection. They put me on two antibiotics and took out the catheter, since it can cause UT infections. Instead, they used what is called a Condom C.

It made a difference. The next day, when Staci arrived, she remarked how good I looked from the day before. I was awake and responding to her. I even puckered my lips to give her a kiss when she leaned down.

Furthermore, I was even better the next day: quite alert, and working with the PT and OT girls, Lauren and Rosie. Staci says they were sweet and cute, and she hoped I could notice that (I don't remember them). When Staci came in that day, I was sitting up on the side of the bed. They had helped me up, of course. My neck and shoulders were so weak, I could hardly hold my head up.

Staci would sit bedside me and read. Before she left each time, she would massage my arms and legs. We got the best news one afternoon: they were going to move me out of ICU and onto the first floor. The new room was decorated and furnished like a hotel room, with a great view of the patio outside. Cottage Hospital is a wonderful place, and we were thankful.

*

The rest of the month continue my progress at Cottage Hospital. On the 25th of September, Rosie and Lauren were able to help me stand! The nurse called Staci to tell her—she was so excited.

My fever went up a bit one day, but the white cell count was normal. The nurses said it was nothing to worry about, it was just part of the normal healing process.

Finally, on the last Sunday in September, they took out my tract (breathing tube). This was a considerable step for me, and it also meant that I had healed enough to be able to move to a facility nearer to home in Camarillo. Unfortunately, with the level of care I need, I don't qualify yet for any of those facilities. Staci and others continued searching for a place that would take me once I regained enough strength to begin a full rehabilitation workload. For now, it was better to keep me in Santa Barbara—easier for my Dad and all my coworker friends to come see me, and Staci was used to the drive and didn't mind. We determined that I would move to Mission Terrace Hospital in the Rehabilitation Program, which was nearby.

On the last day of September, I was cleared to leave Cottage. Staci said she was a bit sad—she was there every day for seven weeks, and everyone had gotten to know us. Even in the cafeteria, people would stop her and ask how I was doing. It was a home away from home, and I could not be more grateful for all the people at Cottage Hospital. They are true angels of mercy.

Mission Terrace/Cottage Rehab (October)

Staci collected all my belongings for the trip to Mission Terrace. An ambulance took me there. While I was still not completely aware of everything going on, Staci was not happy with the new place. It is so different from Cottage—not as well-furnished or peaceful. And it appears that I am the youngest person in the place. Staci left me there feeling quite uncomfortable.

The next day, she talked to Denise, my care manager, who talked her through it and helped her become more comfortable with the place. When she came in to see me, the nurse had given me a shave and put a regular t-shirt on me. Staci thought I looked great! This helped her feel better about Mission Terrace.

I have a roommate now, and his name it Tom. He is quite nice and easy to be around. Staci made sure to introduce herself to everyone, letting them know she would be here each day. She also made sure to speak to the PT, the OT, and the speech therapists, to discuss the goals and expectations. Of course, she stressed how much she was hoping they would get me well enough to begin doing regular rehab.

The doctor called Staci later, to assure her I would be well taken care of, and that they were ordering her a chair for my room! Someone had apparently told him of Staci's concern about the new place, so they stepped up —an encouraging sign.

The next day, Denise said she had pulled some strings and gotten me a bigger room, with plenty of room and the chair for Staci.

*

At my new place, the visits continued. Besides my sister, mother, and father, other friends, and, of course, Staci and the kids. Unfortunately, my mother and Staci were still arguing about who could see me and when. I also had frequent visits from my brothers in uniform. I remember a K-9 deputy visited with his dog. He thought the presence of a dog would make me happy, and it did. But the deputy did not realize that the dog was a bit rough, and it nipped my hands and arms while playing with me, and caused me to bleed a good bit. Since I could not speak, I was unable to tell him or anyone else. I am sure the nurses were not happy after he left when they came to check on me.

Despite the promising words and actions from the staff, it did not go well at Mission Terrace over the long term. Staci felt they were not feeding me enough. My Dad would comment that he could see my spine—I was not getting the nutrition I needed. I still had a feeding tube, so there was no reason for this.

With Staci's frequent complaining, and me not being able to talk and tell them that I was hungry, it became a problem. Eventually, one of the nutritionists was fired over the issue. While this resolved that issue, Staci was not happy with me being there, and she began begging the doctors and others to find another place for me. Eventually, she prevailed, and I was moved to Cottage Rehabilitation Hospital in Santa Barbara. This was associated with the Cottage Hospital that I had been at first, owned by the same corporation, Cottage Health. It was specifically designed for rehabilitation for people with brain and spinal cord injury, stroke and stroke-related disorders, musculoskeletal dysfunction, chronic pain, and other neurological and complex orthopedic conditions.

Staci was thrilled with this change because, even though it wasn't the same hospital, we'd had a positive experience at a sister facility.

*

Becoming aware of myself and realizing that I had a stroke was a stunning reality check. I had to re-learn basic things, and nothing in life had prepared me for that. Learning how to eat, how to talk, how to breathe again was a nightmare. My memory of this period is still fragmented, and funny things will still pop into my mind. I recall that I disliked one of the nurses. I remember being so worried that I was wearing Depends diapers. Once, the diaper I was wearing was wet and bothering me, so I ripped it off, making a mess. Then the catheter came out and I urinated all over the bed.

Although the overall facility was better, one of the first nurses who cared for me seemed to dislike me for some reason. Perhaps that was just her demeanor, and she was like that with everyone. I could not use the toilet yet at the time, and so I wore adult diapers. She would leave me in soiled diapers all day long. Wet with urine, I would tear it off. The gel in the diaper would leak out because I ripped it, and along with urine, it was a total mess. I had no trashcan to put it in. She didn't check it often enough, and I had no way to communicate my frustration to her. It was quite humiliating.

I begin to call her "Nurse Ratchet" in my head, but I could not voice my frustrations. Thankfully, I was moved to a different room, and things were better. Still, I felt like the nursing staff avoided me. Was I a difficult patient? Was it just me being in a difficult situation and being negative? I remember, or example, regularly pushing the button when I needed assistance to be transferred to a wheelchair so that I could go to the bathroom, and it seemed like they would take forever to respond. Perhaps I was angry and difficult, but surely, they were used to people going through such a life or death scare and not being in the best of moods.

There was a night nurse who I noticed was very kind and sweet to everyone except me. At least, that's how it seemed. Again, I had no idea what I had done. I didn't think I was being a bad patient. She would even come in and take the candy from my nightstand that my family had left me when she thought I was asleep.

Yet, there were some wonderful staff as well. I remember one of the staff collected rocks at the beach when he was not working, and he would bring them to me. He would come in and show them to me, just a little view of the outside world that I had not experienced in what seems like forever. He was also an excellent cook and had a great personality.

My mother and sister came to visit me almost every day, and they would encourage me and help me if I started to slip down in the bed and could not get myself up. I have to let them know through using hand gestures, almost like charades. I know it was difficult for them, and the nurses because I am 6 feet (1.83 m) and four inches tall.

I began therapy. I used an alphabet board to communicate. The doctors did not think I would ever be able to speak again. I would try to say a word or two, but not a sound would come out. It was so strange, and difficult to explain. Something that I had done without thinking for decades just didn't work.

I used hand gestures—like charades—to communicate. While that might be a fun parlor game, it was incredibly frustrating as a way of life. My speech therapists used flash cards with pictures to help me. Still, not a sound would come out. The therapist would tell me not to get frustrated, but all I wanted to do was speak. It seemed like such a simple thing! Why couldn't I do it?! I would be thinking about a word—how it looked, how it sounded, what it felt like to say it—but nothing came out. Doctors said maybe a Voice Box would help. I didn't want that. I wanted to make a sound!

When I couldn't talk, along with all the other things I was unable to do, I wanted to end my life. I had *never* been a person to feel sorry for myself—yet here I was. My first speech therapist was named Kim, and I communicated some of my frustration. I didn't see the point of going on. But Kim kept working with me, helping me to talk agin.

She took care of me and talked to me about suicide. She got quite upset about it, telling me that I was not the kind of person who gives up. It worked, and I renewed my intent to be able to talk on my own someday. (As often happens in such situations, I fell for her. She was an important person in my life who helped me through a difficult time.)

Then one day, it happened. I made a sound. It was such a little thing—nothing to most people—but for me, it was like winning the Olympics.

Eventually, I could speak and be understood. I didn't need a Voice Box. I was talking on my own! True, it was still difficult, and it did not always sound clear or understandable. But I could speak!

It took a lot of work and time, but improvements were coming. I'm still working on it, it's a challenging process, but the alternative was not an option in my mind.

Even today, though, communicating is one of my big frustrations. Something that was so easy now takes work. I realized that the labor involved in speaking often made me not share things that I would have otherwise. It was just too much work. When you see the bewilderment on your children's faces because they cannot understand what you are trying to say, it is heartbreaking.

I learned that it helped to think about what I want to say, go over it in my mind, and then try to speak it. I know that, typically, that made me seem dumb or slow. Such a simple thing should not be so difficult.

My size also creating a problem with the bed. I was uncomfortable almost all the time, so at me and air bed, which was longer. I was so excited—until I found that the bed was so loud, and it never shut off. All night I would wake up to it whistling and keeping the mattress firm. It was also supposed to make it easier for me to roll over, but for whatever reason, it was more difficult. I requested my old bed back.

I begin going to "eating class." It seems strange that one would need a class for something so basic that infants can do. But when your body no longer works like it should, it is necessary to learn how to eat with disabilities and not speed food all over the place. Still, it was difficult, and with multiple plates on a tray, it was inevitable that a plate or a utensil would fall to the floor.

Every Thursday we had group sessions with the doctor. The doctor had us discuss the accident that caused our injuries. One man said that he had been working in security and was hit by a car, which broke both of his legs. He was very large, and I started laughing. I knew it was inappropriate, but I couldn't help myself. Other people started laughing, too, and then I could not help myself. The more details he told, the harder I laughed.

The doctor gave me dirty looks, but I just could not stop. I don't know why, it was just a funny image to me. Maybe it had something to do with my condition.

Fundraiser

In 2014, my friend Marc Hammill, who has been on the SWAT Team with me, organized a giant fundraiser along with the Sheriff's Office for my medical expenses.

On February 14, 2015, they held an event with food and a silent auction. So many generous and compassionate people got involved to organize and promote the event. Many others got involved, donated, cooked, and helped in so many ways: police and sheriff's offices, local fire department and the local government representatives. SET (Special Enforcement Team) set up a gofundme page to also help, which raised more than $30,000 in less than two weeks.

The event was far more than I ever expected. I was stunned and moved by the outpouring of support and care. Friends (and people I didn't even know!) were involved—not only police, firemen, and paramedics, but celebrities, family members, high school buddies, people from my gym, and so many more. It was overwhelming.

In the midst of a very difficult time for me and my family, I was overwhelmed by the generosity of kindness of people. I could not express the debt of gratitude I felt. It was a blessing that gave me some encouragement and kept me going. Even today, I can think back on that and get a warm feeling in my heart.

Coming Home

You might think I was so ready to get out of rehab and back home. Yes, part of me was quite ready to get out—but another part of me was scared. It was the fear of the unknown. I would not be going back to my old life. I would be embarking on an almost entirely new life. The only thing the same would be my house, my wife, my kids, and my family and friends. And, as I discovered, even some of those things were about to change, much to my surprise and shock.

My needs were extensive. All I could do for myself was ear, drink, sleep, shower, and use the bathroom. I was worried about my wife and kids, but was powerless to do anything for them. I felt so alone in my misery and my situation.

Furthermore, I required support and guidance in this drastically new life, but had a lot of trouble finding it. And perhaps sometimes I was unwilling. Therapists came to the house, and I disliked them. I felt like they were pushing me too hard to do things I wasn't ready or capable of doing yet. All the things they told me and asked me to do felt overwhelming. Maybe I just wasn't mentally ready yet. One doctor I met with was a psychiatrist I called the "fart doctor." I called him this because during the session as I had with him, he passed gas constantly. But it felt less like a counseling office and more like I just went in to get a "bank loan"—I was just another customer for them to speak with for an hour and then pay them.

Because of my condition, I could not climb stairs. So I stayed in one of our rooms downstairs, while the rest of the family's bedrooms were upstairs. It made me even more lonely and desperate, feeling so isolated from, everyone. It made me angry. Staci put a baby monitor next to me, so she could hear if I needed help. It was so demeaning and miserable for me—once a strong, big, first responder, and now almost as helpless as a toddler.

Sometimes Staci didn't hear the baby monitor, or it didn't work, so I would bang on the wall. I began to feel like I was trapped in this body that would not do anything I wanted it to do. Once, Staci was trying to help me walk and we both fell, and I fell on top of her. We both laughed because she was trying so hard but could not do it, even though I was so much skinnier than I had been. For years, I was an important person in the family and the community, and now I just felt like a burden. I *was* a burden, and it felt worse than anything I have even experienced. It seemed that my life was slipping away slowly, and there was nothing I could do. It was a dark, dark time.

I am confident that Staci was trying, but it was new, difficult, and unexpected for her, too. My mom and sister would come over and help, but none of us knew how to deal with a stroke victim and the aftermath—including me. This new and frustrating territory began to weigh on everyone.

*

One morning, my daughter was putting makeup on, and she somehow pulled a muscle in her neck. It was bothering her so much that she thought she had really hurt herself. So her grandmother took her to the doctor to have it looked at. This freaked out my daughter because she thought he would adjust her neck and she'd have a stroke and be like her dad. She was finally able to calm down when she realized it was just a minor injury, and it would heal on its own.

It is remarkable how a traumatic incident can affect people deeply, so much as to cause panic and anxiety even when there is nothing really wrong. It killed me to see my daughter suffering and in fear needlessly, merely because she had witnessed what happened to me.

*

I began to feel like my wife was losing any desire to be in the home and help me. It felt like she only did the bare minimum to help me, only when it was absolutely necessary. I figured she'd rather be around normal happy people, at parties, having fun. The police department asked me to take an early retirement. My kids were growing up and more and more out of the house, and it made me feel like I was losing them, too.

There was a time when I thought it would be better for me—and for everyone else—if I just ended my life. The physical effects of the stroke, the marriage and family problems, the loss of my coworkers and belonging to a community…it was overwhelmingly depressing and disheartening. If I ended it all, I would be freed from this debilitating horror, and my wife, kids, and family would be free of it all, too. I simply did not want to be around anymore. I had always thought that suicide was a "cop out." But now, I gained a new understanding of people who find themselves in that situation. You really do feel like it might be best for everyone, even though that isn't true.

I had a pistol upstairs, and I begged Staci to leave it downstairs, and I would take care of the rest when everyone was gone. Of course, she wisely refused.

With no other option, I began to think and ponder. I realized that the people I leave behind would suffer, even it didn't seem so. Suicide might seem like an autonomous act, but it can be extremely difficult for those loved ones left behind—leaving them to deal with a trauma of their own. It was a revelation for me—both understanding why people are drawn to suicide, and also the knowledge that it is not the way to go.

*

It became a routine during the day that Staci would tell me she needed a break, and would drop me off at my mom's house. I knew this was the beginning of the end of our marriage, and it depressed me even further. As this happened more and more, she began bringing some of my clothes along to leave with my mom. I began to feel she wanted to be around me as little as possible.

I understand it is difficult for people to know what to do with someone in my situation. If they are not careful, if they get overwhelmed, they begin to think of someone like me as less than human. My feeling didn't matter any longer. It is true that I needed to suck it up and work harder to get better—at least as good as was possible for me. But I needed my wife and others to step up, especially at first. I have heard other people who have gone through trauma tell me that you find out who is really there for you and who is not. It is a stunning realization, and it is not alway the people you think who will help, and those who give up on you.

Fortunately, my mother and my sister did not feel that way, and with their help, I did begin to make some progress. They helped me meet my needs and gave me encouragement to keep going.

I did not want to give up, but I knew the road ahead was long and rough, and might not be all that good. The feeling of being an ineffective husband or dad was a tough pill for me to swallow. I learned that I had to realize there are many things I cannot control. I had to learn to let them go, to accept that I had little control over my own life now. I have always been so active, healthy, and independent. Now I am sedentary, weak, and thin, and entirely dependent on others, It is a daily struggle—even today.

I began to reflect on my life before the stroke, and came to believe that I was not always as I should have been. I noticed that I had needed a lot of attention from others, and often found it in the wrong places with the wrong people. Staci and I both failed each other, even before the stroke, and had the stroke not happened, we might have just gone on like it had been, perhaps divorcing after the kids left home. Who knows?

This does not mean that I was inattentive. My wife and our kids were most important to me—especially the kids. That's still true today. It is ironic that now I know how to be a better man, but I am less capable of showing it and the spending time. For example, before the stroke I bought a new camping trailer, so my family and friends could go on trips and enjoy each other and could join and bond more. I ended up selling it to another Cop and his young family since we could no longer use it. Selling the trailer was no big deal, but all of life's changes were.

We've all heard inspirational stories about innovative doctors and cutting-edge cures. But the outcome of any massive stroke is quite bleak. Most people die. Others linger for a while and die. Any recovery will not come from some magic pill or innovative doctor. It will come from self-motivation and not giving up. There is a movie entitled *Brain On Fire*, about a girl with severe brain injuries. The girl and her family are frustrated with the doctors and the lack of a diagnosis other than she needs to be in a psych ward. The medical professionals have given up. Then, a talented doctor figures out what is going on with her brain, and devises a treatment. The girl begins to recover and there is great joy and his skill and the results.

Yet, that is fiction. Sure, it sometimes happens, but quite rarely. My prognosis from the doctors was "Permanent and Stationary Disability." It's a pretty dire and depressing diagnosis. Of course, hearing that was difficult, and it depressed me tremendously, and the disheartenment even led to moments of wanting to end my life. I had almost died, was forced to retire, lost my mobility, my marriage was on the rocks. Needless to say, I was suffering from clinical depression. I kept thinking, "All I did was go to the chiropractor for a minor adjustment in my neck—and my entire life changed forever.

Those emotions are natural and understandable, but I knew I couldn't stay there. It would be a waste of time, and feeling sorry for myself did not make me better, and it certainly wasn't better for those around me. Now, I know that I beat death, I got back to my own life (out of rehab or a facility), and if I can do that, I can do anything, Maybe I won't succeed, but that's okay. The goal is to keep trying. Simple tasks are hard—because for me, they are no longer simple! I had to tell myself that even accomplishing those things is huge for me. As I noted before, the doctors said I would never speak again, yet here I am, able to communicate with my voice.

Slowly, I began to realize that it did no good to complain and feel sorry for myself. That changed nothing—in fact, in worsened it. I still cannot believe all this happened to me, and I do sometimes find myself in the dumps once again. But I know that the only thing that will make my life better is to move forward as best I can and to do everything I can to improve myself. We can't control the things that happen to us, but we can decide how we will respond to them.

Divorce

Staci and I had been married for 14 years, beginning on February 17, 2002. Books that I have read state that relationships tend not to survive a severe change or health status. But I was not prepared for it at this point in my life when I needed someone so desperately.

I knew our relationship had changed. Because of the stroke, my retirement, my physical condition, I was already in a bad place mentally and emotionally. I felt hopeless. Even thought our marriage had become difficult, and I knew she was unhappy having to take care of me, I never thought it would end in divorce. Not now. I thought we'd figure it out. We'd talk it out, we'd get better, we'd go to counseling.

After a while, though, I began to suspect she was done with me. She desired a normal life—with friends, parties, freedom, and a man who wasn't so limited physically. Staci began complaining that she needed a break and had countless things to do, and it would be easier if she took me to my mom's apartment for a couple of days. These begin to happen more and more often, for longer periods of time.

I still didn't think it would come to divorce.

One of the most frustrating things for me was that I began to review my life before the stroke—what kind of person I had been, as I mentioned above. I realized I had a lot to learn. I wanted to be a good person, but like many of us, I did not always succeed at it. I had opportunities to cheat on my wife because I liked the attention, but it was wrong. I knew it at the time, of course, but now, with my entire life at stake, I wanted to be better, even though in some ways, it felt like it was too late. So, it is likely, I thought, we would have divorced eventually anyway. But at this point I felt the worst for the kids because, before my stroke, I think we would at least have waited until they were out of the house. Still, I can now say that for all the bad brought on by the stroke, I learned I needed to be a better person and began to work on it. It shouldn't take such a trauma to make us wake up and grow, but that's what it takes, sometimes.

I got up the courage and talked to Staci about it. She was surprisingly understanding about it, as we both had not been the best for each other, even before the stroke. It was painful. Another blow in a series of blows to my life.

*

About a year after I came home, my caregiver came in and handed me divorce papers from my wife. It was surreal for me, and I sat, looking at the papers, unable to believe it. Staci didn't even come to me herself and tell me, another terrible blow. A stroke, a severe disability, months of hospitals and rehab centers, an invalid living in a home, forced retirement, and now this?! It was hard not to focus on how I could have been a better husband and a better dad, with the regrets and depression that come with looking back on a past you cannot change.

We separated on September 1, 2015, about a year after my stroke. Dissolution was finalized on October 27, 2017.

It was a series of challenges that I was completely unprepared for, and it was a dark, dark time for me. I was heartsick for myself, but also for my kids. They had a dad who had almost died and would never be the same again, and now they have to deal with divorce?

I know that Staci did not mean to hurt me, but I felt like I was going through hell—my entire world had crashed in on me. Just as I was struggling with trying to make something of myself and move ahead, I'm hit with a brick in the head.

We both had regrets and today we have moved on. She failed me at the time, but she is a good friend now, many years later, and I know she is a good person and cares about me. Our kids are doing well. I know the stroke was traumatic for everyone. It is still a balancing act.

I was fortunate to have some good friends visiting me, and some good nurses and others. Having been through so much already, I knew I had to keep going, I had to rethink my life *again*. I had to remind myself that all of us were doing the best we could in a horrible situation, with no good answers.

But I knew I had a long road ahead of me to attain any sort of normalcy. Here I was, a strong, independent man now laying in a dark room, disabled and helpless with a baby monitor! They say Hell comes after death, but this felt like I had already arrived. I helped people my entire adult life, but now I was in need and living a nightmare.

I know my ex-wife sees things differently than I do about our divorce, which is not surprising. She says she felt more like a "caregiver" than a wife, and that we were headed down different roads, whereas I felt abandoned by my life partner. But I know it was a difficult situation. The stroke was life-changing for both of us, and I know that she loves me and did the best she could, and I will always think highly of her. I do miss being married to her at times, but I know I had to move on.

On My Own

Stacy began dropping me off at my mom's house more and more often, and began bringing belongings with me, I realized that I was going to be living with my mom. I felt like I was with a babysitter, at 44 years of age.

My mom was wonderful and helped me out a lot. Still, I did not expect to be living with my mom. Just another humiliating and frustrating setback. Once a big, strong, police officer, I was now an invalid living with mom. It was just another terrible blow to my life that I had to work through.

At first, we were in a one bedroom, one-bathroom apartment. It was not easily accessible or designed to handle a wheelchair. We called maintenance to install push bars and ramps. My mom slept on an air mattress, so I could have the bed. We had many wonderful and entertaining conversations about many things—both small and large, meaningful and trivial. We laughed and we cried. As difficult as the time was on me, those are happy moments I will never forget. Her neighbors at the apartment building were quite nice, and often gave us movies on DVD to watch.

Of course, I needed help with eating, changing clothes, bathing, and transferring me from my wheelchair and back. I did not want any help, of course, wanting to do things on my own as any grown man would. But I had no choice. I simply could not do it myself at that point. I had to allow the help, and, as an independent person, it was a humbling experience.

My mom and sister were helping me around the clock, doing the best they could in these difficult circumstances. But both of them worked, and I knew I required more support. I found a caregiving company that could provide the necessary care, who had the experience and strength to handle my severe situation.

Finally, in 2018, I found a new apartment that was only a block away from my mom. My own place, but close enough for her to still help out. At first, I would give her money for groceries and the bills. Eventually, I began to take care of those things myself. The simple task of grocery shopping for myself was a major victory for me.

*

Like many people, I was guilty of unfairly judging some disabled people before my injury. Then I became one and my eyes were opened. I learned a lot I did not know. There are approximately sixty million people in the U.S. with some form of disability, and over a billion world-wide. My disability was from a stroke, but most are birth defects or results of illnesses of some sort.

Throughout the decades, a number of individuals and organizations have pressed to pass some bills to help the disabled. The goal, of course, is to find ways to help the disabled live as normal lives as possible in a world not built or designed for them. Things that I had never paid attention to were suddenly crucial, if I were to accomplish even the most basic things, like getting into a building or a vehicle. Nothing about a disability is easy, and, of course, I would like for all accommodations to be made in every way. Of course, the problem is sometimes that such accommodations can be costly or difficult to implement for many public places. I don't have all the answers, but I do know the difficulty of trying to live without some reasonable accommodations, at least.

When I moved into my own apartment, I had to use some dirt to make a slope leading to my apartment. The office eventually put in a concrete ramp, as they had promised when I moved in. It took about three months, but it made the normal comings and goings from my apartment *so* much easier.

*

Imagine feeling independent and efficient, then suddenly you move very slow, and even the most basic tasks are challenging. Moreover, you are acutely aware of how other people see you and treat you differently, even though your person, and your mind have not changed. I often feel like I am being patronized, which I understand, but it gets old and frustrating. We are all influenced first by what we see, and it fixes concepts and ideas in her head. We can't easily see past that into the mind, attitude, and personality of another person. And this is typically difficult to explain to people. This just adds to the amount of loss and grief that I have experienced. Perhaps the biggest loss for me is the loss of my independence. For so long I did everything myself, I felt competent and resourceful, intelligent and handy. Now I must depend on others for even the smallest things. At the beginning, I couldn't even feed myself or wash myself. I had no choice but to learn not to let it bother me. Not to care. This is part of the process of healing physically, mentally, emotionally.

I have learned about myself that I don't care a lot about what people think, and even more so now after my stroke (I'm not speaking about those who are closest to me that I love, of course). Yet I do care how I come across to people, and I want to avoid being a jerk. But not worrying about what people think is very freeing!

This experience also made me realize that some of my relationships were not built on a strong foundation, and could not survive my condition. Some of that is my responsibility, of course. But it's just the nature of relationships, that some of them are stronger than others, and you often don't know which is which until crisis comes. It makes me sad some of the relationships that I have lost, on the other hand, the clarity of whom I can trust and believe in is comforting.

Trusting someone was always hard for me, but now I have to trust people to help me in so many areas of life. I often think that being an officer didn't help me in some ways because you get used to people not telling you the truth. Many people want to avoid getting in trouble, so they lie, or they obfuscate. Getting used to this sort of mistrust in a job unfortunately translates to real life. I know this is a problem I must work on because it is a leap of faith for me to believe someone's intentions are pure. I sometimes worry that my work on trust has come too late in life, but better late than never. I am learning to trust, receive assistance, and appreciate it with thanksgiving.

I've also discovered that I have some abandonment issues in addition to the trust issues. It is true that some have abandoned me, but I cannot apply that to everyone that I know and meet. The times that I have wanted to trust someone and have been disappointed loom large in my mind, making me more guarded. I had to realize that my go to was to not trust people. This is no way to live, and I want to become more trusting while not being naïve. It is a constant battle to learn to love and trust others when deserved, which also applies to myself.

Often it merely comes down to me just wanting to be her. Just being paid attention to, taking seriously, and being communicated with is so meaningful. Since my stroke had a serious effect on my speech, I know this makes it more difficult for people to do these things. They have to pay more attention to my mouth and my lips, and my sounds, in my facial expressions, which is not a normal thing for people to do in life. It is very frustrating for me, as I'm sure it is for the people who interact with me.

Losing friends, especially close ones, is painful. Yet often looking back, I can see that the relationship had its problems anyway, whether in communication, or mutual respect, or whatever it might be. I'm working on learning that my stroke actually gave me more clarity about the people that I can trust, who I want in my life, and who do not deserve to be there. By the same token, it has forced me to face my own flaws, and hopefully has made me a better person and a better friend to those who love and care for me. I needed to let go of those friendships was difficult as well, I had already lost so much! But I begin to think of it like cleaning out a garage or a house, to make way for a new life.

Caregivers

Throughout my rehab and beyond, I needed the help of several caregivers. As I mentioned before, I am quite independent and take pride in doing things for myself. So requiring help and being dependent on others has been difficult for me. At only 50 years old, I would love to have independence, but of the prognosis does not bode well, for that goal. Every so often, it seems like the last independent decision I made seven years ago was to visit my chiropractor for some pain relief.

Some of my caregivers have been great, but others drove me crazy. Finding good ones is not easy, and requires trying them out and getting to know them. With every new caregiver, I explained my situation, my personality, my needs and how I wanted to proceed. Some understood perfectly, whereas others seemed to misunderstand or were just stuck doing things the way they always did. The best ones are hard to find and hard to keep because they *are* so good, and therefore in demand.

I have always enjoyed my alone time, which I had little of while in the hospital and in rehab, and it was still in short supply once I came home. It is not that I didn't appreciate all those who helped and wanted to help (both caretakers and family and friends). But I wanted to work on being able to do things for myself, to give myself a sense of accomplishment and less dependance on others.

Letting others control my life was a difficult pill to swallow, yet we all need help at times, and I needed a lot. I learned quickly that resistance is not helpful at all, and that sometimes, letting go is valuable and even therapeutic.

The best caregiver I had was also my personal trainer. After meeting her, I was pretty sure she was going to be excellent, but I did not know for sure until we had worked together for a while.

One of the things that happens is being able to do even little things become large goals and moments of frustration. Having a woman put lotion on my back, or put on your socks and shoes might sound nice, but when you can do so little yourself, you'd rather do those things yourself! And yet, I had some caregivers who could not do even those things well or consistently.

Once, the company sent someone who could hardly speak English. How can I communicate my needs when we can hardly speak the same language. Imagine having a stranger sent to your house to care for you. I had speech problems and could not speak well at the time. She couldn't speak English. What person at the caregiver company thought that was a good idea? It's like the blind leading the blind! Two people who have communication issues.

Another time, a caregiver failed to show up. No call, no text, just didn't come for her shift. It made me so mad, I wanted to tell them never to send anyone again. But I can't do that because I can't survive without the help. You can imagine the call I made to the company.

Some caregivers try to become your friend, or at least it felt like that. Maybe they saw themselves has counselors or therapists as well, and felt like I would be helped my developing some personal closeness. Well-meaning, perhaps, but someone hired to be your caregiver should not also be a friend. There are too many conflicts of interest—money the most crucial one. On the other hand, some caregivers were so distant and unpardonable, as if they were just going through the motions, and I was hardly even a human being to them. Boundaries are important, and not all of my caregivers were good at the balance.

Some tried to do more than required of them. Nice sometimes, but not always a good idea. One of my caregivers wanted to help me out my changing the oil in my car, install a new electrical outlet in my bathroom, and even do my exercise routine with me. It may sound harsh, but what I needed was someone to help with medication and some basic caretaking needs. The rest I needed to learn to do myself.

It is a difficult balancing act, and for me, it was the constant presence of caretakers that was so hard. Imagine having a sort of adult babysitter at age 50, with you at all times of the day and night. Every so often, I just waned to be alone for a day!

It also requires a lot of trust to have a caretaker with you at all times. Being a police officer did not help me in this area because we were always on the lookout for people lying, deceiving, and stealing. It made it difficult for me not to be suspicious of anything that seemed out of the ordinary. And yet, *everything* I was experiencing was out of the ordinary. I was frequently at a loss as to how to handle it, and I know sometimes I did not handle it too well. But I learned some things about myself, and how to sometimes, and just for others.

For example, I realized that I have a stronger personality than most. By that, I mean I usually speak my mind, and I realize that I wasn't always kind about it. I wasn't trying to be unkind, just direct. I've always paid great attention to details, so much so that I've wondered if I'm not a little OCD. That can be difficult for people to handle occasionally. When I was a training officer at the police academy, I found that most people were not like me in terms of details. Yeah, I think this was why I was a good officer: I could notice a hair on someone's jacket, or a little nervous tick. My hearing has always been acute as well, and I found myself watching shadows and reflections, to see what people were doing. Perhaps that is excellent in the work that I did, but it is not always helpful when having to rely on others in your personal life. I had to teach myself to try to be less observant, or ignore some things going on.

At the same time, in my profession, I saw many people taken advantage of by people they trusted. Housekeepers, employees, elder care, all of these positions can lead to the more unscrupulous people taking advantage. Usually, it was financial motivation. Life can be difficult enough, but when you discover that someone you trusted is taking advantage of you, it is a terrible hurt.

I am convinced that my experience in my job made me more suspicious of caretakers. I had some great ones, but unfortunately, some of them were less than honest, which didn't help my suspicions.

Sometimes, I would have to make accommodations. Yes, I needed help, but no one was inside my head and could read my mind or understand my intentions and desires. I tried to give more information and direction than necessary, and hope that my communications and interactions would be better. But none of that would help if the caregiver could not be trusted, even with little things (like stealing the candy that my family left for me when I was in rehab).

As I write this, I have just fired another caregiver. I had a hard time understanding this. My caregivers had two free hours per shift to do whatever they wanted, plus I could be fairly flexible in the work schedule among the different caregivers. That seems like a pretty good deal, but maybe I don't see it from their side. My experience was that finding a good one was not easy, even with the help of the agency that helped me find people.

I tried to find the balance between being firm in what I needed, while trying to be understanding of others.

I remember that I had a friend's retirement party to go to, and the caregiver would have to drive me about an hour to get there. She kept mentioning that she was worried if we left the party too late, she might not be off by four when her shift was supposed to end, I didn't understand why she couldn't make an exception for something special. I finally got so frustrated with her complaints that I asked her to take the rest of the day off and not come back, she was dismissed. I'd figure it out myself.

I certainly don't want to be part of the problem in this difficult situation, but it was often frustrating, and I knew I had to strike a balance without being taken advantage of.

One morning, one of the caregivers asked me if I wanted to use a "sippy cup" instead of a normal cup. Did she see my like a toddler? I am sure she was trying to help, but to me, it was a hurtful comment on my condition. Didn't she know I wanted to do as many normal things as possible—even if they were difficult? And I know the answer is, no, she was just trying to help. Another example of the difficultly of being so limited after a long, normal life.

Similarly, I once had a good friend who was working for me. She had needed some work, so I hired her as my a personal trainer. One day, after she had been working with me for about two years, I asked her for a phone number of one of her family members, so that if I had an emergency, I could call. For whatever, reason, this sent her over the edge, and she quit immediately. I don't know what happened, and everyone has their difficulties, but this weighed on me for a while.

I should also mention the issue of having family work for you. The idea that you should never have family members as employees is an adage for a reason. Yes, these are people who hopefully care for you, and are willing to go above and beyond. And yet, it is a difficult balancing act with conflicts of interest. Depending on family continually, with no end in sight, can be difficult and can come with a price.

My son has done a good bit of caregiving for me, a couple of days a week. Of course, it's wonderful to be with him, and he wants to be helpful. Yet, he is still young, and occasionally, he gets a little complacent or even impatient. Being 18 when he began, he's on his cell phone a lot, and he likes to tease me. I hired his girlfriend and him to help me because he needed a job and I thought I would be helping both of us out. Blurring the line between father, child, and caregiver is tough for both sides, and yet at the same time, with good communication, it can be something that makes your bond even stronger. It is certainly a test of a relationship, one that my ex-wife and I failed. I had the best of intentions, but I did not know the pitfalls of the blurred line between father-child and patient-caregiver. It resulted in some arguments, and I realized later, it was unfair of me because he didn't know anything about caregiving. He was willing to try for his dad, and I've that I was appreciative.

Relationships Changes

Relationships are difficult even in the best of situations. It doesn't matter whether they are parents and children, or siblings, extended, family, friendships, or romantic relationships. They take work and patience.

I learned that having a stroke, makes them even far more difficult. My parents and family of origin were quite helpful, but my condition did change things. Suddenly, they wanted to coddle me again like I was a small child. Understandable, of course. But we all had to do some adjustment.

Friends react differently, depending on their personalities, situation, and the closeness of the friendship. Some simply did not know how to act or what to do. Many of these simply stopped talking to me. Others were quite helpful in the beginning, but as they realized, I was going to be this way for the rest of my life, they slowly distanced themselves. A few good close ones have stayed with me in a new sort of relationship from the previous.

Many of my friendships were quite a blessing, and I even developed new friendships, of course. One of my caregivers, a 60-year-old woman from Chile, became a friend. She is a great person, her faith was strong, and she has a 28-year-old daughter that she loves very much. I have so much respect for her and her life, and for what she has done for me.

Romantic relationships are even more difficult, as you might imagine a different level of intimacy in intellectual, emotional, and physical that doesn't exist in other relationships.

I have been married twice, and I actually found being married easier than dating, even though both marriages failed. Men and women are different in so many ways, and yet we have so much in common and need each other. Some of the most important events in my life involved, some remarkable women alongside me, supporting me, helping me, and being my partner.

At the same time, I can see some benefit in being single. There is less drama, there is enough work to do, and being able to come and go as I please, and not having to answer to anyone is helpful. This is especially true with a lot of the challenges I have had. It gives me independence and freedom. And yet, the loneliness and the need for another person to hold us accountable, to love us, and to help us through difficult times, to enjoy life with, is something I have been missing.

In my career as a police officer, I think I handled over 100 domestic disputes. Alcohol was almost always involved in the most serious and criminal situations. Usually, the man was the aggressor if the dispute was between romantic couples. I often found myself frustrated that women would stay in a bad situation. Yeah, I came to understand that sometimes what you know is easier to handle, even when is, it isn't good, then, heading out into the unknown alone if you end the relationship. I get it, but it is still dysfunctional, and it would frustrate me a lot.

In my new situation, dating was quite difficult. I am in a unique situation, and there are good and bad things about it. I was excited to date again, and perhaps have the company of a woman and enjoy our relationship, but I found immediately that the challenges of my new life also made that difficult.

Like most people, I have not always been the best in my marriages or other relationships. I've made terrible mistakes. But I have learned a lot through my new situation. I've tried to be honest with every potential romantic relationship since my accident. I try to let them know what I can, and can't do you, what a relationship with me would be like, especially the more difficult areas. And yet sometimes that torpedoes the relationship right from the start. But if I don't tell them certain things, that can come as a surprise later, and cause the same kind of problems. Sometimes I think I'm better off single. I would love to have a partner that I could depend on and trust, but finding that person would be difficult because they would have to be unique, considering.

Learning the lessons that I have learned, both before, and especially after my accident, I've taught me a lot. Most of the lessons were very difficult. I have learned to have compassion for myself, and not be too hard on me, but I have also learned to have compassion with others, who simply cannot handle my situation.

My girlfriend (the caregiver from the hospital) and I went to Las Vegas on a trip she had won. She is seventeen years younger than I, with great energy, and a wonderful way of dealing with my health issues and shenanigans. She pushes me to get better every day.

She had correctly answered the question to win the trip: who was the famous boxer that appeared in the film "The Hangover"? I was quite excited about doing something that felt somewhat "normal."

The trip was all expenses paid for a few days. It turned out to be quite an adventure! We were required to attend an hour-long presentation about purchasing a timeshare. While we were not required to buy anything, we had to stay for the entire presentation, and it was a hard sell. I don't like these kinds of pressured situation's to purchase something, so we left. We thought about just going back home, but decided to stay at another hotel and pay for the trip ourselves.

If that had been the only frustration, it wouldn't have been so bad. But one night we were heading to a show and running late. In our haste, she was pushing my wheelchair, so we could go faster. As she was pushing me on a ramp, she lost control and stopped, but the wheelchair kept going! I should have warned her that this could happen. I ran into a glass door with a loud crash! Fortunately, the glass didn't break, and I was not injured. But I was quite embarrassed!

Not only that, but we needed to have some clothes cleaned. The hotel had a service, so we put our clothes in the provided plastic bag and turned it in. When the clothes were returned, the bill $200!

Needless to say, what I thought would be a fun getaway turned into a trip with numerous frustrations. Yet we are a great team and we're always having adventures!

*

People often say "be honest with me," but I've learned that, sometimes, when I'm truly honest or forward with people, they leave. Maybe my delivery is wrong, but think sometimes people would rather not hear the truth. When I was an officer, I was honest with people, and they would usually listen to me. That isn't always true in personal life. These days, it feels like people dismiss me and just think, "he doesn't know what's going on." I know it is hard for people to look beyond the speech impediment in the wheelchair, and to see me as a smart, competent person who just has physical and speech difficulties. People look beyond the speech impediment and wheelchair, I'm a pretty smart person. We all engage in "judging a book by its cover," and that is certainly easier than actually getting to know someone, unfortunately.

Before my stroke, when people didn't listen to me, I would just blow them off. But now I find much more frustrating, especially when it is something important. Nothing has really changed, except that communication is far more difficult for me. But communication is a big part of interacting with people and relationships.

So I have learned not to always be brutally honest. I don't intend to hurt anyone's feelings, but I also want to be honest. Even little "white lies" bother me, even though I know it's merely a small and truth to avoid hurting someone's feelings.

When I was an officer, I could be brutally honest, but in retirement, and in personal life, it is not always the best technique. I have learned to be more careful with peoples feelings.

While the physical challenges that I have experienced have been incredibly difficult, and a lot of work, there is also been a lot of self reflection that had to be done. My kids have told me that I was sometime a jerk before my stroke when I was an officer. This stunned me because I thought I was always a nice guy. Sure, I knew that the kind of job I had sometimes hardens people, but I thought I was above it. I tried hard to maintain my friendships outside law-enforcement, do in that line of work. I found that it was hard for people to understand what it was like to be a police officer, like many other professions, and so my closest friends were often other officers.

Being honest with yourself and others, that's became difficult and challenging, even more so than before my stroke. Admitting to myself that my life will never be the same again is a challenging experience, as it would be for anyone.

This has been one of the most difficult things for me: trust. Maybe I expect too much, but I have found it almost impossible to find reliable, trustworthy people. Is it something about me? Is it my attitude? Some combination of both? I have been truly at a loss. I find myself regularly disappointed with others, including my own friends and family. I felt that way occasionally before my stroke, since then, it seems to have become more frequent that people let me down. Is it really worse than it was before? Or am I blinded by my circumstances, which lead to some negativity? Yet I don't feel that way about everyone because I do feel like I can trust my sister, and usually, my mom.

It isn't that I don't recognize other people are trying. Perhaps I am setting myself up for failure in this area because I am so dependent on others, far beyond what I ever expected to need. After my stroke, I wanted someone that I could confide everything to. Someone who would believe in me, it would be there every step of the way.

And then I read that, and I think perhaps I am asking too much of people because I am in a unique situation and require more people can offer. After all, they have their lives, their struggles, their relationships, and their responsibilities.

The good thing about this is that it made me realize that in the end, the only thing a person can do is believe in themselves and trust their own actions and opinions. It's really up to us. Sure, it's wonderful to have someone that you can totally trust with your innermost feelings and emotions. Someone who will put up with you when you are at your worst, and enjoy life with you when you're at your best. It is also a two-way street: such a person would also need me to do the same for them, and I'm not confident that I'm always capable of doing everything that someone would need because I am limited.

Perhaps that person exists, and I will find them someday. And of course, learning to depend on yourself, and fighting through it as an individual, is wonderful for personal growth. But it can be very lonely.

There are times when I find myself sulking and wallowing in my misery. Even at the time, I knew it's not healthy and only makes things worse. It can take a while to get out of that mindset, and it is a terrible, dark place to be. If you have experienced such suffering, you know exactly what I am saying.

When I find myself feeling sorry for myself, I listen to the song "I'm just a kid" by Simple Plan. It helps to know that others have felt this way. I'm not really alone, this is something that other humans have gone through. A therapist said once, "feeling sorry for yourself is like giving free rent in your brain." You're allowing those negative and unhelpful thoughts to take over. I find myself thinking that I *do* have a lot to feel bad about!

I look around society today and see some terrible attitudes people have towards police officers. In any group of people, you're going to have some bad words, but that doesn't mean the thousands upon thousands of police officers are people with evil intent. I often feel sorry for my ex-colleagues, and consider that perhaps I am lucky that I have missed this period of time when police officers or a target rather than someone you depend on. Thinking about such things in society, and there are a lot of negative these days, makes me even more discouraged.

These are the times when I must focus on the positive things rather than the negative things. It is not always easy, and yet I do have a lot to be thankful for. It is at these times that I know I need to do something like write down all the positive things about my life. The good career I had. The wonderful kids who are part of my life. The people who help me and check on me. Unless I can do something about the negative things in my life, there is no reason to focus on them.

Moving Forward

In college, I went to a counselor for some personal and marital issues. I learned a lot of valuable life lessons. The counselor seemed genuinely interested in helping me—not merely giving me ideas or advice, but asking questions of me, helping me find answers on my own, and answering my questions when I had them. I think of him now, and the impact he had on my life, not knowing that I would need everything I learned to get through this traumatic change. I gained insights into myself, tools on how to look at life, and how to view my problems and faults.

One of the things he really helped me with was to be kind to myself. To realize that, despite my flaws or mistakes, I am a good person. You have to love yourself, you have to forgive others, if you want to have a meaningful and good life. Once, he asked me, "have you ever heard the phrase, 'cultivate your shit garden'?" I had not. He explained that we all have 'shit' in life—from our own doing, but also things that are not our fault. There might be a tendency to just complain about it, sit in it, and feel sorry for ourselves. Or, you can use that 'shit' as fertilizer, to help you learn and grown and bloom. It's your choice—cultivate that garden!

I don't think I fully understood what he meant by that phrase until the aftermath of my accident. Now I get it. Failed relationships, serious health issues, the physical difficulties of my life—I can find ways to use those to make me a better person: stronger mentally, with more compassion for myself and others.

In addition to learning to be kind to myself, and tending my own garden, I also learned that forgiveness is key to a good life and a good attitude. Harboring anger or pain because of other people or unfair events only makes things worse. And it does not solve anything or make us feel better. It allows us to move forward, remove the negative emotions and energy, and it demonstrates grace to others.

I always believed that it was important to be positive at all times. To be negative and critical was rarely helpful.

My accident and resulting life challenged those beliefs to their core. I had difficulty, at times, thinking anything more than "my life is a disaster, and it will only get worse. My life is over."

My counselor recommended a famous book called *Man's Search for Meaning* by Victor E. Frankl. It's an inspiring story about a Jewish psychologist who was a survivor of the German concentration camps during World War II. He made notes for the book while imprisoned. He writes about the mindset of survivors versus that of those who did not make it. In his opinion as a psychologist, those who had the greatest odds of success in horrific situations were people had some hope, even though it was a dismal experience. Having a positive attitude is difficult enough for most of us in traumatic times, but add starvation and the fear of death, and it becomes almost impossible. Frankl wrote that if a person can find *some* meaning in suffering, they on their way to surviving. It is meaningless suffering that saps the will and strength from a person.

Imagine having a small piece of bread in your trouser pocket, so you have a "treat" when you get so hungry you can hardly think straight. My situation was—and still is—traumatic, but nothing like what those men, women, and children experienced in those concentration camps. I visited the Holocaust Museum (the Museum of Tolerance in Los Angeles) a few times, and I still have trouble wrapping my brain around the evil of what happened to these people. What they experienced is a reminder of the terrible trials that so man people endured. It makes me think, if they can survive that, then I really don't have anything to worry about.

I have always been a "people person." I loved meeting people, interacting with strangers, spending time with family and friends. Likewise, I was active and enjoying so much life has to offer.

My accident made all of that almost impossible. Often, strangers don't know how to act towards me. Friends and family don't know how to help, or are so uncomfortable they limit their time with me.

I had always assumed I'd be healthy and sound. When simple physical things became difficult—and sometimes impossible—I did not know how to handle it. Everything I had taken for granted had changed: where I can live was limited (for example, stairs were impossible). Would I ever be able to drive again? Was I trapped unless I had someone to take me places? Even then, I would have to schedule with them and work around their schedule? Relationships became much more of a challenge (and they are already challenging for healthy people). How would not being able to work affect my finances? Even speaking for a little while exhausted me.

The stroke had impacted everything in my life. If I had been older and retired, perhaps it would have been easier. A bit more expected at the end of life, perhaps? It's still challenging, of course. But at my age…

There was also some tremendous regret. Not only that I did not appreciate what I had more, but how I viewed people with disabilities. I did not know the overwhelming difficulty, and I did not know how different the exterior and the interior of a person can seem. I supposed that people with disabilities weren't intelligent, merely because of their slowness and difficulties interacting or doing simple things. How ashamed I am now! In my mind, I am the same person I have always been. I know that—but people don't know that. Even those who knew me before see me differently, even though my mind and my person are unaffected.

It has taught me that we should never base our judgments about people on how they look or talk. I suppose we all know that inside, but it is difficult not to let it affect our attitudes. How I wish I had known this before—I would have been far kinder and more intentional in my interactions with so many people.

It is not that I don't attempt to be positive. I worked hard at it, and failed so often. As many readers will know, when depression sets in, it is a deep and hard battle. It takes over your mind, and getting out of it is one of the hardest things a human can do.

I tried to remind myself that for a long time, I could not speak at all, and the doctors did not think I would ever be able to without a mechanical voice box. I would try speaking, and nothing came out. I tried and tried—nothing. But now I can speak! I did it!

One day, I went to a dental appointment, and I got to talking to the hygienist. He asked me how I maintain such a positive attitude, joking and smiling, after all that happened to me. I explained that I focus on the things I can do—make my own challenges. I work on eating clean and doing as much physical exercise as is possible for me. I work hard to stay positive.

Of course, I have my bad days, like everyone. And I don't have all the answers. All I know to do is after each setback (mentally, emotionally, or physically), is to get back up on the horse and keep trying.

Today, I try to listen better to others, and get to know people for who they are inside. I work not to let the outward affect how I view them. The regrets are strong, but I tell myself that I have learned a valuable lesson about what it means to be human, even as I am often treated as less than human myself.

I had to learn to hang on to things like that. Victories are important, even when they are little things like merely getting around or drinking something on my own.

*

During my career in law enforcement, I used to train officers how to do pursuit driving, along with such things as the PIT (precision immobilization technique) maneuver to end pursuits. (This is a tactic that uses your vehicle to force the other car to turn sideways abruptly, which makes the driver to lose control and have to stop. It was a lot of fun.

Today, I usually need a driver, since it wouldn't be safe for me to drive. I remember that I went to the DMV because I needed an ID card, and I had to take a written test and do an eye exam. The DMV decided I could get a license since I passed those tests. I remember thinking, "is this really a good idea?" Apparently, being in a wheelchair, unable to talk clearly, and other physical setbacks weren't enough to keep me out of a car. This was crazy to me, but who am I to question the DMV?

*

There is a song by the band Metallica called "One," which is about a war veteran who cannot speak, and has no arms or legs to help communicate. Although some circumstances are different from my story, I certainly related to the story in a way I would never have before. Especially the concept of being a prisoner in your own body. Imagine trying to explain something to someone, but you're unable to, and they are trying their best, but cannot get it. It is difficult not to get angry or frustrated, yeah, yet that would do no good.

I've always thought I was fairly competent and intelligent, and that has perhaps sometimes led me to seem like a know-it-all. I understand that, but I do think I at least have basic skills, perhaps better than most. I have accomplished some difficult things in life, and excelled in a career that can often take a lot of work, courage, competence. So, to have difficulty with things like brushing my teeth, or paying my bills, which are now as difficult as some of the most difficult things I've had to do in life, is difficult.

Every so often the reality of my situation hits me anew, and I am overwhelmed. I work hard at my mindset and the tasks I set for myself, but occasionally, I need an escape. Sleeping, watching movies, and working out are ways that I battle the beast of being overwhelmed.

Some people dislike being alone, but I have never had a problem with it. I think it is important to be alone and comfortable with yourself—it is a good discipline.

*

Another of the things I've learned how to be almost indifferent to some of life's hurdles. Of course, the things that truly matter— family, relationships, mental and physical health— are significant. But I have noticed that we, as humans, often tend to "major in the minors."

That is, we tend to sometimes focus on things that we cannot do anything about, or are really not that critical. They may seem like it at the time, because of the emotion connected to it.

I noticed this in myself. I would become so concerned and anxious and stressed about things that, in the big picture, didn't really matter. I would ask myself, "will this make a difference in a week, or a month, or a year?" And often the answer was "no." Yet, when you are in an emotional state, it is often hard to remember that. Practice makes perfect. Keep going. Being kind to yourself when you fail in this, knowing that it is a long journey, and there will be setbacks. My goal is to take two steps forward for every step back. I want to be able to look back a year ago, and say, overall today, I am better than that person. I have grown, learned, and matured since then.

Focusing on the Positive

As I have mentioned, I found myself frequently going down dark paths in my mind. I knew I had to stop that way of thinking, or at least find a way to lessen it. One of the things I begin doing, was to look around at my life and try to find positive things. At times, it was quite difficult, and I would say to myself "There is nothing positive!" But I knew my mental health depended on it. That might sound difficult, and it is, but I knew my mental health depended on it. So, I would try to find anything positive.

Some of the ways I did this might seem somewhat strange. For example, I would focus on the idea that at amusement parks, I am allowed to go right to the front and avoid the lines. I can park close to every place I go, because of the handicap placard on my vehicle. Those are positive things that make my life easier. Sure, I would have taken the inconveniences and not the disabilities— but that's not my situation.

When I was in college, I worked for a glass company. I saw plenty of car wrecks that had seriously injured occupants. I didn't imagine at that time that I would someday be a first responder to such events. One of the memories that stood out for me, however, happened while on a delivery run. I spotted a horse with his leg stuck in a wire fence. I stopped the truck and hopped a couple of fences to try to extract the animal. I put my shoulder under his body, bracing myself to push up his massive weight, and was able to free his bloody leg. He bucked, making a lot of noise, as if he was delighted to be free. I felt happy, too, having done a good deed that day to help the poor animal. Today, I think of that story, and believe that you never know what's going to happen. In any situation, you might be able to make a difference, whether a person or an animal. So, I know that I can still make a difference in people's lives—and maybe even another horse!

Once, my girlfriend and I were driving, and she made an illegal U-turn. A police officer pulled her over and came to the driver's side. As soon as he saw me on the passenger side, he greeted me kindly and asked how I was doing. We talked a short while, and then he gave her a warning and told us to be careful.

Perhaps the same thing might have happened had I not been disabled and still a police officer. Maybe. But he would certainly have given me a hard time. "Come on, Dan, you know better than this!" He might even have been angry for us putting him in that situation. Perhaps he would have told the boss or given us a citation. I choose to think he just offered a warning because her illegal turn did not cause danger to anyone, and he thought I'd been through enough without adding something else, as minor as it would have been.

*

Communication is still one of the greatest challenges. Even in the best of circumstances, communication can be difficult, especially when you are trying to portray detailed or philosophical ideas. It's easy to communicate "I need water" or "It's too hot in here." But try communicating some complex feelings about life, or relationships, politics, or entertainment.

I have noticed that people tend to be a bit dismissive when you cannot communicate clearly. As if you aren't as smart or aware as other people. I used to think that about disabled people! Now I get to walk in their shoes, and have discovered that it just isn't true. Sometimes, such people have greater insights into life, what really matters, and purpose. The saying "the broken are the more evolved" spoke to me. I have learned something new about people, and can treat them more compassionately now. Another positive!

Sure, it is frustrating that I didn't learn that lesson until I had a stroke. A high price to pay for insight! I tell myself that I didn't have control over that. I can only control what kind of person I am. And this insight can make me a better man.

*

Most of us are aware of the disorder of post-traumatic stress (PTSD). This is where a past trauma continues to affect one's life, even though the trauma is over. The classic example is that of a soldier coming back from war. A door, slamming or another loud sound can cause them to fear for their lives, and dive for cover.

I have certainly experienced PTSD even before the stroke. Being a police officer required me to be on some pretty traumatic experiences, that left effects on me, just as it does for many police officers who are active in the field. High suicide rates, alcoholism, drug use, and burnout are common. Add to that some small and larger abuse directed at law enforcement exacerbates it. Being called a pig (or worse), racist, and the recent moves in some areas to defund us, as if we are the problem, all contribute. During some of the more difficult times in my career, I would think to myself that I should've been a firefighter. Everybody loves them!

For a long time, the fear of having a second stroke, exhibited itself as PTSD. I would feel a slight pain, or a twist, and panic would set in. Couple this, with some of the more minor PTSD from being a police officer, and I could find myself thinking very negatively. As an officer, people lied to me regularly. During my recovery, I felt abandoned by many people that I cared about. My defenses would go up and I would criticize others.

But I knew that was not the way to move forward. If I was wrong in the past and hurt people, that I need to admit that and ask for forgiveness. If others have robbed me, I have to try to understand where they're coming from, and even if I can't, I need to forget them and move on.

A Final Word

The medical and therapeutic term "plateau" refers to the point at which a patient reaches the best they ever will. Opinions differ on how long that takes and at what pace, depending on several factors, of course. The word can have a bad connotation because it has the idea that once you "plateau," you will not experience any more improvement, and, in fact, will probably get worse over time.

I don't like the idea of reaching a point where you just throw in the towel. I prefer a more positive attitude. Sure, it is difficult when someone doesn't appear to be making progress, or a new obstacle arises, whether it be physical, dealing with insurance, and everything else about life. My approach is this: I will continue to push forward in my life and in therapy. I will find ways to improve myself until the very end. Perhaps I have reached some pinnacles (just like I did in my prior life), but I do not intend to give up or "plateau."

There are many things a person in my situation can do that might surprise people. Sure, I do a lot of physical therapy and speech therapy to improve myself. I'm not satisfied with my current state, even though it is more than the doctors ever thought I could accomplish.

But I also work out three times a week. I enjoy rock climbing and paragliding. Recently, I went up in an Ultra-Lite plane. We had to attach my feet to the foot pegs with duct tape because I could not keep them still. No problem—I still went up in a plane!

I've gone paragliding in Santa Barbara. It was quite challenging without my wheelchair, but I did it. And the weather and scenery was beautiful!

*

I have never wanted to be seen as a complainer or as negative, and yet in the condition, it's hard not to sometimes. But I do hope my story will help readers appreciate what they do have in life rather than focusing on the negative. Because you never know, how things might change. There is no guarantee, in the phrase, "there, but for the grace of God, go, I" is genuine and worthwhile.

I also hope that it helps people realize that no matter how difficult things get, you can handle it. One bit at a time, one piece at a time, you do your best to stay positive, and deal with each little thing as it comes along. Try not to think of the big picture because it becomes overwhelming; focus on the task at the moment. That always helped me.

All major studies show that stroke survivors have a significantly shorter lifespan. The damage to their body, plus the resulting effects, such as being in a wheelchair, also play a role. Surviving the stroke itself is a massive challenge, but dealing with the constant fatigue of just trying to live can also be overwhelming.

Stroke victims experience different degrees of results. Some lose their life immediately or soon thereafter. The other end of the spectrum is a mild stroke and the victim returns to a normal, or nearly normal, life. My stroke put me in the middle of the spectrum. I often lament the fact that. Could not have been one of the mild ones, who recovered quickly. Yet, I know that I am fortunate not to have been farther up the scale. I was young and healthy, and the stroke only affected my motor skills and speech. Not talking well and being in a wheelchair is hard, but I keep working on it and moving forward. Isn't that how life is? We encounter obstacles, and we can feel sorry for ourselves, or give up, or make the most of it and keep fighting. I've done all three at times! But today, I mostly focus on the last option—I decided that I will refuse to quit! Some people say life is a test, others believe this life prepares us for the next. Whatever the reality, life remains interesting to me. There is always something to work on, always something new to learn, always a new challenge—even if you didn't have a stroke. How we respond to adversity matters more than the adversity itself.

I know I have done better than the odds would show. I survived, something that might not have happened. Not only that, but I can speak now, something that the doctor said I would probably never do. But I would be lying if I said that it is not difficult to know that I will most likely die sooner than I should, and that I am afraid.

Despite some regret from my past, as we all have, I would not change my memories for anything. Even after the stroke, I've had a lot of personal growth and experiences.

I stay busy. I have always liked challenges; I just needed to reorient my thinking to realize this is just another of life's challenges. Sure, I did not choose it like I did other challenges in my life. But it is a challenge, nevertheless: a chance to learn, grow, and enjoy life.

Laughter is an important part of my mindset. Whether it is funny people, comedy shows, or comedic movies, I know the importance of laughter. And part of that is being able to laugh at myself as well—I am quite capable of doing some dumb but funny things!

Everyone has a cross (or crosses) to bear. This is mine. To say my life has been a struggle is a considerable understatement, but I have so much to be thankful for. I have never been too religious, but this experience has been life changing. I realize surviving the stroke was a miracle.

I have my frustrations, as I have outlined above, but we all do. Mine may be a little different, but that's okay. We deal the hand that has been dealt to us (some of our own making, and some not). It is not about the challenges we face, or how successful we are. It is about our attitude towards it.

Often, I think there is not much in life we can control. We kid ourselves that we have control over much of our life. But I do know this: I can control my attitude, mood, and actions. It isn't always easy, but the goal is to keep at it.

Over time, I found it very frustrating to have to deal with the constant adjustments in my life that I had to make. Coping with regular things in life is a constant battle of trying to find better, easier, and more comfortable ways of doing everything. And I mean everything, from personal hygiene, shopping, to relationships, to washing clothes. All the things that a person takes for granted— that I took for granted— are now major projects and readjustments. I've said, I often thought it would be easier just to give up. But that is not who I am, and this is the hand that I have been dealt.

Over the years, I have discovered that, like everything else, the harder I work at it, the stronger I get. Adversity makes a person more resilient. You tear down a muscle to build it back up stronger. I can get my head around that. It is all the loss and grief that comes with it that is a struggle. I lost my marriage, some close friends, a career I loved, and the self-respect that comes with all of that. I work to find a way for my life to be meaningful and with purpose. I believe it's actually important to be able to have meaning and purpose regardless of your situation. But this lesson came at a massive price.

Looking back, I can now see how complicated and chaotic my life was. I was so self-absorbed that I didn't realize my dysfunctional behavior was bringing down those I loved. I've made some poor decisions in the past. I believe it is critical to take a good honest, look in the mirror, and face, what we've done, and who we've been. To take ownership of both the good and bad of our decisions. It's alarming to look at all the mistakes, and one has to muster up a lot of courage to face it honestly. To not make excuses or blame others.

I have pledged to take personal responsibility for my actions, and be respectful to others, no matter what. To me, that seems like the path to self-respect, but more importantly, to meaning and purpose in our lives. What I've learned is that it is not good enough just to identify the mistakes in the heart I caused, I have to find a way to act on it. To deal with the past in a healthy way, and then move on, lessons learned. Not to beat yourself up over things you can't change. To apologize and make up for hurts caused if possible and appropriate. Some of the greatest challenges in life, have the biggest lessons to learn, and help us grow more than positive lessons.

Occasionally, I see life as a big experiment, that we are all involved in. What will we learn, and what will we do with what we learned? What happens if we change this, or if we change that? It's much easier to go through life without thinking about these things, and just almost live on autopilot. But it is not the best life.

I look at myself today: I was a law-enforcement officer, and now I am in a wheelchair. My life is drastically different today in every way. I began to try to consider life to be this experiment, or variables are thrown at me that I must look at from all sides, and figure out the best way to handle it. The positive way. The healthy way. To make myself a better person, and to make the world a better place for others; however, that might be possible, even in small ways.

This means protecting yourself as well, however. Learning to say no to things. Learning that, perhaps some people are not the best for us, or us for them. And especially learning not to beat yourself up for past mistakes. Once this mindset is in place, we can begin to turn to being a better person, a better friend, a better dad, whatever our roles might be.

My experience has been eye-opening and life-changing. I've learned many important lessons that I needed to learn. The way that I had to learn the lesson, I would not wish upon anyone. But it is a lesson, nonetheless, and one that I am grateful for.

And that is the primary lesson that I have learned. No matter what your situation, what's been done to you, or the terrible mistakes you have made, you can find ways to be thankful for what you have. It may not be much. It may not be as much as you used to have. It may be difficult, and sometimes you may want to give up. But there are always things to be thankful for, even if it is just the beauty of a sunset, a drink of water, a roof over your head, or a bit of time with a good friend.

Be thankful in all things as much as you can, and you will find joy in life, even in the worst of situations.

Reality is everything. To be continued…

About the Author

Dan McSkimming was born in Sant Barbara, California, and spent his life in the area. He obtained a degree in criminal justice from Sonoma State University, followed by an internship with the probation office in San Francisco. His decision to go into local law enforcement led him to work in a couple of juvenile halls and for Nordstrom in the loss prevention department. After completing police academy, Dan served as a police deputy for eighteen years and was a member of SWAT (Special Enforcement Team) for thirteen years with the Santa Barbara Sheriff's office until his stroke. He lives in Southern California, and refuses to permit his physical limitations to stop him from remaining active.

If you feel generous and have a couple of minutes, please leave a review online where you purchased the book. Thank you in advance.

About the Publisher

Sulis International Press publishes select fiction and nonfiction in a variety of genres under four imprints: Riversong Books, Sulis Academic Press, Sulis Press, and Keledei Publications.

For more, visit the website at
https://sulisinternational.com

Subscribe to the newsletter at
https://sulisinternational.com/subscribe/

Follow on social media
https://www.facebook.com/SulisInternational
https://twitter.com/Sulis_Intl
https://www.pinterest.com/Sulis_Intl/
https://www.instagram.com/sulis_international/

www.ingramcontent.com/pod-product-compliance
Lightning Source LLC
Chambersburg PA
CBHW032128090426
42743CB00007B/506